Foreword by the Bishop and the Lord Mayor of Coventry

This book brought back to us many memories as we read it. For us, as for many in Coventry and throughout the world, the fiftieth anniversary of the Coventry blitz marks a significant memorial to the harrowing hours of that one moonlit night.

We found the book fascinating and very moving. These accounts by ordinary people, often during or soon after the terrible bombing, are moving and remarkable. The stories are simultaneously absolutely marvellous and absolutely dreadful.

After the bombing of Coventry, Provost Howard, in his Christmas broadcast from the ruins, spoke of a determination "to try to make a kinder, simpler, more Christ-child like sort of world in the days beyond this strife". In Coventry's saddest hour, as in one of its most joyful days since, this surely is the same genuine message of our city and of this book; the struggle for the hope of a new humanity, one human family beyond nationality, race and class.

That is why it is good for us to look back with the help of this amazingly vivid record to the terrible experience of that night in November 1940, and to find in that appalling tragedy and its aftermath a strange ground for hope. As the Provost has said of his walk through the ruins of the Cathedral shortly after the blitz, "One tremendous fact stands out clearer than any other and forms the central theme of this whole history. On the night of this destruction, in an amazing and miraculous way, Coventry Cathedral became the living embodiment of the tremendous truth that, through the crucifixion and resurrection of Jesus Christ, all crucifixions in human experience can issue in resurrection."

Nearly fifty years later John Sillett, the manager of Coventry City FC when the club won the FA Cup, looked out of the window of the Council House onto the vast, multi-coloured throng filling the streets of Coventry as far as the eye could see, gathered to welcome the Sky Blues back from their great Cup victory. "If you look out of the window, you can see all colours and all creeds," he said. "We are all one now. If we can keep that going in this country, it will be a wonderful thing." Old Coventrians said they had not experienced that kind of unity since the war years and the blitz. Then also, there had been the same sense of oneness which our society and our world needs so much today.

We both retain vivid memories of the war years. For the Lord Mayor, especially.

"I shall remember the firemen and other air raid services who fought so heroically to stem the tide of fire and the flood of injuries and deaths. I was in London during that night, serving with the 1st Battalion, London Irish and I clearly remember standing at Stockwell tube station, listening to all the German planes going over and wondering which poor souls would be getting it that night. A few days later, like many others, I read with dread the story of the blitz and stared in amazement at the photographs of George VI in the ruins of the Cathedral.

"I had my share of wartime memories and sadness. I was at Dunkirk, helping the evacuation and saw a destroyer blown up nearby by a dive bomber, killing most of its crew. I watched the dogfights over the fields of Kent during the Battle of Britain and witnessed the horror wreaked on London during the Blitz, with all the homeless, grief-stricken people and the crowded tube stations at night. After joining the Parachute Regiment, I was dropped over the Rhine, where we landed amongst a German Panzer Division. The war was terrible for us all.

"I joined the fire brigade and was posted to Coventry in 1946. Even then, the city centre was still a scene of devastation. It had not been rebuilt, but was a panorama of rubble and dereliction. The shops were temporary, there was no precinct, and you couldn't buy a house anywhere. My wife and I tried to find accommodation, whilst I biked twenty miles a day from Fenny Compton.

"What impresses me most about this fascinating book is the detail of what people said, their history, telling us what it was like. For those who have been born since, they too will find it fascinating. As an ex-fireman, the problems the fire service had most impressed me. They ran out of water and tried various ways of getting supplies : from the canal, from ponds, anywhere. Fire Control was put out of action and the machines couldn't get through the cratered roads. Perhaps the most telling fact was the call for a hundred extra fire pumps. Usually, for a bad fire we ask for five extra, so a hundred was quite extraordinary.

"One thing at least came out of that night. It was the resolve of people, both in and beyond Coventry, to meet and increase their understanding of each other. City twinning came directly out of it, the first being with Volgograd, devastated by the bitter fighting in its streets. Young people from Dresden came over to help clear the Cathedral ruins. My own daughter went to Dresden for two years under the Coventry Council for International Understanding and helped plant a peace garden there. Coventry is now twinned with twenty-six cities from all parts of the world, many of which have suffered similar devastation. The city has also been involved in international peace events, notably peace conferences at Hiroshima and Nagasaki. It is a founder member of the World Union of Cities for Peace."

The Bishop was at school in Dunchurch at the time of the raid.

"I was taken out to see the glow of the fires which rose from the burning city. Soon afterwards, I think it was the same night, I was huddled with other boys in a shelter when a bomb was dropped from a plane unloading spare high explosive after blasting Coventry. It landed so close and with such a terrific bang that the explosion threw me off my ledge in the shelter, into the air, and covered us all with dust. Later in the war I went up to London. I remember the criss-crosses of sticky tape on the bus windows and the rush into the shelters before a raid. I remember the doodlebugs as they ominously droned overhead, the sudden spluttering into silence, the dreadful wait as they fell and the loud crash as they blew up. I learnt to recognise the throbbing moan of the German bombers and witnessed the huge fleets of American planes like enormous armadas going over in the last period of the war to do more terrible damage to Germany than had ever been done to Britain.

"I can recall quite vividly the atmosphere of everyone coming together, in unity of spirit and purpose. I especially remember the packed trains and the atmosphere on the platforms. There was a kind of cameraderie, everyone mucking in together, like the accordion players or mouth organists who seemed to pop up nearly everywhere.

"Since those tragic events, the Cathedral has built links all over the world. Now, we are planning to send out crosses of nails from parishes in Warwickshire to parishes throughout the world, to re-establish those links, especially with Eastern Europe and the 'Third World'. There are crosses of nails in both Dresden and Berlin. And in Berlin they have a similar ruined church, the Kaiser Wilhelms Gedachtniskirche, left to commemorate the destruction of war. There is a tremendous potential for growth in mutual understanding in the world.

"This generation is important as well. This fiftieth anniversary is not just about the war, it is about building a better understanding in Britain today, caring for the poor and deprived in our city now. Helping the young and old, those in need and plight, to give them hope. It is a matter of commitment for this generation to our fellow men and women which is as important. People are isolated more than ever. We are all too individualistic. Somehow, we must rediscover that sense of communal spirit where the people are as one with each other. We must create a new outlook on life, one nation, one world, where we all belong to each other. That message comes directly from the heart of the Coventry blitz experience."

Amid all the horror of that moment, when, with a kind of "stunned helplessness" people saw "precious buildings, homes and loved ones blitzed into blazing oblivion," there were glimpses of courage, of caring, of human sympathy which upheld them through their ordeal. There was an apocalyptic feeling of ordinary life being caught up suddenly into an unbelievable cataclysm. Friends, or members of one family, reacting suddenly to danger found that "one could be taken, the other left". The night sky, lit by flares, became bright as some dreadful day and hailed down fire and destruction. Frail air raid shelters were hit and their occupants killed. Homes fell around them. A bus sank into a crater in the road. Firemen and medical helpers were stranded in the chaos, but still performed feats of incredible, generous heroism. Through it all, like a prevailing thread, holding all the fragments together still, ran a sustaining love, mourning, protecting, reaching out to heal where it could. Even in the final, dazed grief of the bewildered morning after the raid, a father and daughter clung to one another in the rubble of their home, thanking God for sheer survival with inexpressible emotion.

At the height of the fire, as water to fight the flames ran out, Provost Howard, watching the Cathedral burn, was filled with a sudden sense of recognition: "It seemed to me as though I was watching the crucifixion of Jesus upon His Cross". As the blackened spire still stood against the glare, its clock chiming the dread hours, God was still with them all in the tragedy and "His Love was indestructible". The glimpse of that fire as a part of the infinite sacrifice of the crucifixion, was the crucible in which Coventry Cathedral's symbol of the Cross of Nails was forged. This book can give us a fresh discovery of that vision. We can, as we relive that night, enter not only into its tragedy, but also into its inextinguishable hope.

For fifty years since these awful sights and sounds, we in Coventry have been building links of peace and reconciliation. We are helping those countries of Eastern Europe to rebuild their culture, trade and expertise, with our children visiting them as well.

The fiftieth anniversary was commemorated in a host of ways, many of them spontaneous and unco-ordinated, but which add greatly to the official events and prove that people of the city don't want the memory to be forgotten. On the 14 November a Commemorative Service was held, with the invited heads of Coventry's twinned cities and other cities badly bombed in Britain. There was a Blitz Ball, plays put on by the Belgrade and Criterion theatres, a series of lectures at the Polytechnic, a display at the Herbert Art Gallery, others at the libraries, school activities, and an inward city trek to form a ring of light around the city.

This last symbolised the city rising from the ashes and was a reverse of the nightly trek out of the city by people during the blitz. The Lord Mayor can remember that too clearly himself, witnessing people pushing their wheelbarrows and camping out in the fields around Coombe Abbey, and, in the mornings, the bomb disposal teams defusing unexploded bombs. Above all, we shall both remember and we shall be taking what steps we can to ensure such terrible devastation never happens again, but that we keep firmly as our aim the maintenance of peace and the pursuit of international reconciliation.

W Hardy - The Lord Mayor, Councillor W Hardy

✝Simon Coventry **The Bishop of Coventry**

Introduction

As I began to compile the personal accounts and reports in this book, I felt a growing sense of humility. Like most who will read this book, I was not born at the time of the blitz, nor were my parents old enough to join the forces. My mother was evacuated from the East End of London to Wales, whilst my father was struggling through his school exams while helping his father fire watch on top of a church in Paisley, Scotland.

The War had left me cold. Veterans dressing in their medals, memorial services and parading had seemed to be living in a past which, I had felt, was not glorious, but represented the height of man's evil to man. I wished to forget it, look to the future, move on with my own life.

Working on this book has changed that. The suffering and destruction which occured on the night of 14/15 November 1940, on top of the dozens of raids leading up to it, and with the two April 1941 raids yet to come, was so total that it hit me between the eyes. At first, it seemed merely a collection of stories and half-remembered anecdotes, some humorous, many trying to be cheerful years after the worst horror of that night had faded in the memory. But, as I came across records, accounts, letters, the odd scrap of paper recording the death of a whole family, the reality of that dreadful night began to sink in.

I found the compiling and editing of this book a harrowing experience, one I would not wish to repeat. Many of the accounts are stark and describe death and suffering in a way which I found, at times, very hard to come to terms with. The pain of the people was comparable with the worst outrages of the war. Bodies of men, women and small children piled high in the temporary mortuaries, the little girl clutching her doll, her eyes staring blankly into the sky, mass graves, people blown into lumps of flesh, often against their friends and families, the shocking devastation in Broadgate, all became, at times, unbearable to read, let alone write down, edit, and compile.

There are many ways in which we all try to mitigate our sense of loss and our grief. We joke, try to look on the bright side, remember only the good times, say it was all for the best, look to a greater purpose behind it all, believe one was destined to survive simply because one did survive. They all serve to blunt the knife that penetrated right to the heart of Coventry that night.

The truth of that night cannot be mitigated. It was one of the worst atrocities of war. The city was not just bombed; it was destroyed. It was Guernica, but on a far greater scale. It was comparable with the horrors of Dresden, Frankfurt and Cologne, or the towns of the Somme bombarded during the First World War.

So why remember it? Why hark back to the past? Why not forget and get on with life today? Partly the answer is, so that we don't repeat the mistakes of the past, and it is very true that those who fail to learn the lessons of history are doomed to repeat them. So, yes, we must reason why and build structures of peace and reconciliation which will make such an event much less likely. So too, those who went through the blitz must learn to verbalise the trauma of that time, to help them come to terms with it.

But it is more fundamental than that. To "learn the lessons" is still to distance ourselves. We must become thoroughly immersed in the event to understand it. That is the key, **understanding**. We must relive it, experience that horror, that nightmare, have it thrust before us in all its bloody desperation, if we are to realise what our parents went through and why they went through it. We mustn't forget; we mustn't be allowed to forget. It wasn't just a bombing raid; it was survival. Yes, survival of "Our Values", Democracy, Great Britain, The Empire, and so on, but much more fundamentally, the survival of old men, of pregnant women, of nurses, children, babies, road sweepers, clerks and typists. Survival of the poor and the vulnerable.

So the question becomes not, why should we remember, but, why should we recall it in minute detail, uncluttered with theories, opinions, reflections, post-rationalisations, excuses, or palliatives? War is stark; it is full of fear, distress and despair. It was not the city's finest hour; it was its worst. It was not another noble chapter in the Cathedral's history, but its most abject. It was not a time of great community spirit, but one where people were left with nothing else but each other, and rejoiced that they still had that. Let's not hide behind soothing words, but express the terror of that night in its true light, as the people of Coventry themselves witnessed it. The most honest testimony is one of blunt truthfulness.

It is vital that the history of those who have suffered and who are the real actors in history, but who have no access to writing their stories, is remembered. Their history, real history, is often forgotten, and the plain recording of it is the best service we can do.

There are two things I wish to convey in this book. First, to get as close as possible to the details of that night, as far as possible to relive those hours. Second, to get over the emotions of the night, how they changed, built to anger, fear, terror, subsided to silent despair, then rose to the reassertion of life that had to go on.

Wars don't just happen. Politicians, generals, industrialists seem, at times, to have a vested interest in them. It is only by recording the suffering their actions have caused and by making history put them constantly in the dock that we can keep the moral strength to prevent further tragedies. It is the people who matter, their anguish, their dedication, their endurance, and it is the intention of this book to capture that spirit and let it become a constant reminder and thorn in the flesh of any who might think they can win another world war, that "some losses are acceptable", or any other of the calculating statements justifying the belief that such a war would be winnable, or even survivable.

Many of the debates which have grown up around the Coventry blitz have been largely ignored in this acount. They have their place, but not here. Whether Churchill knew about the Enigma code which the Germans used to transmit the message that the target was to be "Korn", Coventry, or not; the blunders around intercepting and jamming the German direction beams; whether the city's defences were prepared, or could have been better prepared; whether more fires could have been put out if this or that had been done; all this does not alter the basic fact that the city and its people were devastated, and ignores the one central issue — the extent of our parents' suffering.

For me, nothing else matters, in the final analysis. I feel we can only stand and join in commemoration. Other "issues" merely obscure the horror. Nothing could have been done to materially alter the events, once they had been set in motion. The one issue is how people have suffered, and to record that in as frank a way a possible, to stand as testimony to what that generation lost.

So, here we have it, in all its gory glory. Man being as inhuman as possible to man. And man, perhaps, will look back on that event and, through reflection, find his soul. I hope so.

Tim Lewis

Acknowledgements

To Barry Littlewood, John Watts, Lorraine Ford
and the staff at the Coventry City Council for their
help and guidance;
to Sue White and all the workers at the
Coventry Reminiscence Theatre;
to David Rimmer and the staff of the Coventry
City Archivist's Department;
to Diane Chalmers at the *Coventry Evening Telegraph* ;
to the staff of Coventry's local studies library;
to Gill for reading the manuscript;
and to Coventry City Council
for making this testimony possible

Photographs courtesy of the
Coventry Local Studies Library
Cover photographs used with permission of the
Coventry Evening Telegraph

Contents

The spire of Holy Trinity rises above the ruins of the city centre

14

First Movement

The air was chill. The moon was brilliant in the sky. The city of Coventry, bombed many times already that Autumn, lay quietly waiting......

Air raid log — 14th November 1940

Thursday 14 November:
18.40 Bramwell on duty.
18.50 Entwistle on duty.
19.05 N° 5 Post reported (Officers Fry & Field).
19.12 Red (Public Warning). Bright moonlight (Full moon and stars showing clearly). [23]

The picture in Coventry was as in every other town in the country; streets in darkness, all windows obscured by various kinds of black-out material, motor car headlights masked so that no beam of light was projected above the horizontal, and those few lights permitted in motor omnibuses were dimmed by a covering of bluish paint. People going about their business carried suspended round their necks, in a small, square cardboard box, or some more elaborate home-made or privately purchased container, the regulation gas-mask or respirator, intended to protect in case of attack with poison gas bombs. These were constantly getting in the way, being lost, or left behind, and were generally considered a nuisance by their owners and everyone else.

Nearly everyone carried a pocket torch and some had white patches on their clothes to increase their visibility when crossing the road. Public buildings were encased in a protective covering of sandbags, and the entrances to shops, public houses and other places doing business after dark were fitted with additional doors to form a light trap, so that no ray of light should be visible in the open as customers came and went. [43]

19.20 Incendiaries from NE to SE, completing circle later from SE to NE all round city. Large fire developed 47°.
19.30 Inner circle of incendiaries catching Cathedral, Palace Yd, Broadgate, Barclays & Owen Owen, all around tower.
19.31 HEs [High Explosive bombs] Corporation St, Foleshill, Radford.
19.32 N° 3 reports fire, Pool Meadow area. Confirmed as Gasometer fire

(Gas [Hill] St).

19.40   Cathedral blazing fiercely. HEs all over and around city centre.[23]

The raid begins

I'd had this feeling for days that something was going to happen and it got stronger and stronger. From Binley we could see that things were bad. I watched parachute mines floating down in the light of the fires. [75]

I had a 'feeling' that something was going to happen, so I told the staff at the hotel not to come on duty that evening.

When the sirens wailed, only my wife, daughter Mary and I were on duty. Within a few minutes incendiaries and bombs were screaming down; Mary decided to make for a shelter in Broadgate.

I had placed valuables such as money and jewellery in a bag upstairs for safety. These were soon lost. The upper walls of the building collapsed through bombs and caught alight. It was impossible to get up the stairs. [28]

My mother had already prepared the Anderson shelter and my twin brother and I changed into Home Guard uniform (ready for the invasion, if it came). We usually had a quick meal and then.......the wait.

My father said, "It's a clear night and a full moon — I've got the feeling we're in for it tonight."

Sure enough, the sirens wailed and my mother and twin sisters made their way into the shelter. My father, my twin brother and I went into the street to do our fire watching. We did not have long to wait for the sound of Jerry bombers, with that peculiar pulsating sound, as if the engines were straining against heavy loads.[51]

Tom and I had just got home from work. It was a car factory that had changed over to do war work, aircraft in the fitting and on the tracks where the cars used to be, and in the trim shop they did the sewing of canvas panels for the trailers. My dad came in just after us from Morris Motors, Courthouse Green.

It was six o'clock. Mum was just putting the dinner out and we were waiting to tuck in. 6.10 and the sirens went. [It was, in fact, at 7.10 pm.] Within no time at all the Luftwaffe was over dropping stick after stick of bombs......

Mum and I filled kettles and saucepans with water and got the candles handy, for we knew from other raids that the electric, gas and water would go off, which they did do in next to no time at all. We had a double bed in the living room because we couldn't go upstairs to sleep, as we had had incendiaries

16

dropped through the roof on previous raids. So we took it in turns to have forty winks. But not on this particular night......

The planes came over immediately in waves, such terrific bangs. One seemed to lift the house up and put it down again. We boiled water on the fire for a drink, just like camping.[60]

Rush to the shelters

We had to be ready to go down our Anderson shelter when my Dad came home from work at seven o'clock at night. My Dad built bunk beds in there for us. He made a wall round it like a castle and it had white and blue flowers on it......

We used to hear the planes come over after the sirens had gone. The guns at the Morris and at Herbert's were deafening. You could hear the whining and whistle of the bombs as they passed overhead. Everyone used to duck their heads until the bombs exploded.[26]

The sounding of the air raid siren brought the blacked out, deserted streets into a hive of activity. From the surrounding streets would come hordes of rushing people; women with babies in their arms, toddlers, and others, in their dressing gowns and siren suits. Their destination, the air raid shelter beneath the Island, Jubilee Crescent, Radford. As air raid warden it was my emotive experience to try and see that these women and children crossed the road safely to the shelter, because simultaneously a stream of cars drove past, dimly lit, bearing the AFS [Auxiliary Fire Service] volunteers to the adjacent fire station. How my heart ached for those women and children torn from their beds, many of their menfolk away in the Services.

The night was suddenly transformed to day when the darkened streets became alight as the Coventry sky was encircled by German dropped flares. It looked as if a large Xmas tree was lit over the city. Apprehensively, we waited for the bombs...... [79]

Nellie Lamberti made her way to the basement shelter under what was then the Rudge factory at Spon End:

It took us all our time to take the children. The youngest one was about three and we had to pick her up when she was asleep and carry her down. We would put her down on the pillows, shawls and blankets and she didn't know a thing until the morning. That's how we went, with our other girl walking behind us with a little bag with the insurance policies in. We used to carry all those things.

But in Spon Street, oh, everybody was weeping and making a fuss because they couldn't get any gas or water. The big pipes that the firemen had had to put the fires out ran all along the tramlines, but they couldn't get any water. We had to go round to somebody we knew in the Rudge that had still got the water tap running and fill buckets……

She describes how "it was heaven for us" in the shelter and how hundreds of people were accommodated within its honeycomb of passageways and side chambers, often packed like sardines, gas masks at the ready, their few possessions hurriedly gathered together before they rushed down for the all- night stay:

They came from Sherbourne Street and all the streets all round: Spon End, Holyhead Road and everywhere. We had to sleep in that the best way we could.

We took bits of old mats and things and perhaps little mattresses and put them down in a row: one row for the men and one row for the ladies; and we slept head-to-head, with the little kiddies in between. Later on, they built little bunks, which took us off the floor. It was very cold and we saw rats running down the corridors sometimes. But we called it a haven of refuge.

It was struck at the side of the part we were in and eventually we could feel the water spraying through where the firemen were playing on it. We were all screaming because every now and then we heard a great thud where another land mine or bomb had dropped somewhere and we used to wonder who had got it that time.

There were families being wiped out all the time. There was a family we knew that lived in Crow Lane who sheltered with us. It was a Mr [-]. He lost his legs in the First World War and they used to have to put him in a wheelchair to bring him down there. He had his wife, daughter, three grandchildren, and his son-in-law. One night they didn't come down. They sheltered in an air raid shelter that the Council had put up for them and they were all killed, every one of them. If they had come down the shelter, they would have been safe. That was awful sad that was, awful sad.[84]

Whilst Mrs I Watson was preparing to take shelter herself, with a few provisions and warm clothes, the shelter at Gosford Green suffered a direct hit, nearly killing her husband:

But for the fact that I called my husband and another resident back to get their tin helmets, they would have been killed too. They were in the Home Guard and it was one mad rush from the shelter in the basement as soon as the sirens started and he caught the full blast of the bomb which dropped on the shelter in Gosford Green. He was standing in the doorway, and just those few minutes saved my husband.[126]

Like darning a sock

I and several other youths living in the Grayswood Avenue area volunteered to be ARP [Air Raid Precaution] messengers and we were based in ARP Post 607, in the garden of the Three Spires pub.

On the evening of 14 November we had reported in as there was a Purple Warning — aircraft in the vicinity. We were told not to go too far away.

A certain Mr Salmons was setting up as a photographer in the Allesley Old Road and he offered to pay us to push his leaflets through the doors in the Grayswood area. So, there we were, stuffing leaflets, when we heard this faint throb of an aircraft engine and, looking over towards Radford, we saw this flare hanging in the sky, then another towards Allesley and another over Broad Lane, until there was a circle of flares around the city.

We left our leaflet delivering and raced down to the ARP post, where the wardens were beginning to assemble, wearing their black steel hats with the white W, and Mr Probert, with his white helmet and black W. Mrs Whitmore was a warden and kept an eagle eye on we messengers, who were inclined, as teenagers, to be a bit wayward.

The sirens were still warbling their undulating warning, then the bombing started and we could hear one drop in the far distance, over towards Stoke, then one nearer and one nearer. You tensed inwardly as you could almost visualise the line of bombs dropping out of the aircraft in straight lines — straight for you!

……This Luftwaffe effort was a perfect piece of precision bombing, for we gained the distinct impression of a sock being darned — straight lines in parallel one way and straight lines across. We now know they were using [X-Gerat], the radio beams converging over Coventry, but nevertheless, it was most accurate and not many bombs fell outside the target area.[63]

The night was so brilliantly lit by the moon that convoys of army lorries coming out of Coventry during the raid dispensed with all forms of lighting. Workers cycling or walking in for the night shift watched as the raid developed around them. One was on his way to the Foleshill railway signal box.

It was a cold but calm, clear afternoon as I cycled along the road from Kenilworth to my work at Foleshill signal box, Coventry. The road was traffic-free and I thought about the night ahead of me. It would be an easy night for me, or so I thought. A trainee in the box was being put through his paces by the Chief Inspector. This would leave me free.

I booked on duty at six pm. At seven pm the sirens rang the warning call. It was dark; it was quiet. It gave me an eerie feeling to know that somewhere up there a dangerous, terrifying enemy lurked. Around us were factories making arms and we were the main transport route in and out of the city. Were we the target for tonight?

It had to happen. The enemy were above us, swiftly, silently, ominously coming our way. Suddenly, I was back in charge of the signal box. The Chief Inspector took the trainee back to Nuneaton. I moved a freight train from the Daimler works to Three Spires loop, to where I hoped would be a place of safety, away from the main line, a sure target.

As the train moved away, the enemy came nearer. The signal box was in darkness from the outside, the windows blacked out the dim light inside. I sat listening, wondering what was happening outside in the darkness. By now I could hear the enemy above. I could hear the bombs in the distance, their whine, then the silence. I put out the signal box light and ventured outside......

The buildings opposite had suffered direct hits. Buildings were cracking, crumbling and falling as I watched. Flames engulfed the rubble. The sky was alight; I could see the dark shape of planes in the sky. Fire engines screamed to the scene to do what they could to retain the flames within the area. I could see fires burning all around me. The rails were demolished: no more trains would pass...... [53]

The familiar swish-swishing of incendiaries on their way down from the bomb racks of the planes overhead and their demonaical crackling as they landed indescriminately on roofs, pavements and gardens was again the overture to this particular raid. Sirens had blown shortly before.

Already the sky was glowing at half a dozen points. Fire! There was something terrifying, yet peculiarly appealing, about an air raid fire to the rescue man.

'There,' I thought, as I drove as fast as no lights on the car would allow, 'will be our work tonight.' I was at my rescue post within two or three minutes, but already those small conflagrations were being fuelled from above. A few HEs, then more incendiaries.

"Going to be a warm night," was the cool comment of my Second in Charge on arrival.

A bomb whined somewhere overhead, but he ignored the crescendo of sound — experience told him it was safely distant — and added, "Sounds like [-] district's turn." It was. [25]

Ack-ack barrage

Planes, enemy planes were overhead all the time. It was a marvellous barrage [from the anti-aircraft guns]. We could hear the shells whizzing overhead and shrapnel falling. Bombs also began to fall. It seemed as though they were concentrating on the Stoke district alone. People from next door came in the small shelter, until fourteen in all were in it. [121]

Ack-ack guns opened up, shells bursting with their familiar crump, crump, and sending slivers of schrapnel scything through the air, making us dodge for cover as one large piece glanced off my tin hat and hit the road.

Suddenly, there was a thud, then sparks showered off the road. A large metal object bounced back into the air, then burst with a terrifying whack just above the houses. Something hit the apple tree in our front garden then rolled towards us across the lawn: it was the nose cap from an ack-ack shell.

By this time, Jerry was overhead. Down came a shower of incendiaries, making a plopping noise as they hit the road. One went through the roof of our next door neighbours' house (its occupants had evacuated to some friends in the country).

Thinking the doors were locked, we burst open the front window to deal with the bomb. My brother had gone to get sandbags and simply walked through the back door. It seemed so funny that we had to laugh. We then dealt with the rest of the incendiaries and used up all our stocks of sandbags.

When the next shower came down, we could not deal with them quickly enough, so those that were burning in the street we left. Quite a number exploded, splashing phosphorus in all directions.

By this time, my friend Arthur Butler, another Home Guard man, had joined us. He suddenly shouted a warning and pointed into the sky. A parachute with a large container came floating down, coming to rest behind a row of houses opposite our local vicarage, at the corner of Cheveral Avenue and Tulliver Street. [71]

Hurricane on a house of cards

It was very early on in the evening and I was standing by the front door when suddenly the whole street was lit up by incendiaries. I ran into the street, picked up a sandbag and threw it over a bomb which was lying in the gutter. That very second it exploded in my face and I was thrown backwards. I soon realised I couldn't see. I heard footsteps running and a voice said, "We must get him to hospital". Another voice said, "I will get my car out". There were few people who owned cars in those days, but I have never found out who the man was to this day. [65]

The strips of adhesive paper which were stuck on windows to prevent the scattering of glass splinters by blast were blown, with the window frame, the front of the house, the adjoining premises, and a couple of houses opposite, into the middle of the next street. Brick built air raid shelters were shaken to pieces by the mere vibration of bombs which fell more than a hundred yards away from them and it was safer to be out in the open than in many of the corrugated iron contraptions called Anderson shelters which were buried in suburban back gardens. Other preparations were on an equally puny scale and, when the testing time came, it was as if a hurricane had struck a house of cards.[43]

12th City Battalion, Home Guard

The motorcycle dispatch riders of the 12th City Battalion of the Home Guard had arrived at their headquarters, Grove House, on the Tamworth Road. A full moon was beaming ominously down as the riders stood in groups outside the guardroom smoking cigarettes or munching sandwiches......

Presently, Vernon Muslin, the Officer in Charge, emerged from the guardroom saying, "We had better get ready men. I've just had a phone call from the RAF plotting room at Keresley Grange and there's a big bomber force heading this way. It could be either Coventry or Birmingham, but they don't know which."

Vernon went inside, leaving his men engaged in animated talk on the probable outcome. Ten minutes later, the sinister wail of the air raid sirens commenced and a sudden silence fell as conversation was cut short, all ears straining for the sound of approaching aircraft as the last, dying moan of the sirens was replaced by an eerie, muted throbbing of engines. Suddenly, all hell broke loose as the anti-aircraft guns opened up, followed by the distant thump of bursting shells.

An urgent phone call from Colonel Pugh, the Home Guard Zone Commander, requested four dispatch riders to go to Spon End Waterworks, the zone headquarters, on standby. Hurriedly stubbing out their cigarettes, four riders jumped on their motorbikes and roared off down the Tamworth Road. As the raid developed, a red glow could be seen over the city, and phone calls in quick succession asked for riders to be sent to key points in the city, such as Livingstone Road Baths, Centaur Road School and many other sub-headquarters.[103]

Firemen soon overstretched

The Yellow Message was received at 19.05, the Purple at 19.08, and the Red Warning at 19.10. Action commenced quickly in the brilliant moonlight, and the first fire was reported at 19.24. Throughout the night there was no perceptible lull in the attack, and the White Message [the All Clear] was received at 06.16 on 15 November.

Within the first five minutes a gas main was fired in the central part of the city, providing a beacon for the early raiders. Fifty-six calls were recorded in the first half hour, and many of the fires called for three and five pumps as *first* attendance, and a few were single pump jobs.

Previous experience of large scale raids had been that fires in the early stages were confined to one or two districts, due to what would appear to have been the result of a straight run across the city. The tactics employed on this occasion must have differed inasmuch as in this first half hour there were fires in six widely separated districts. Fortunately, the local organisation is based on six zones with which the outbreaks roughly coincided, and it was, therefore, possible to bring pumps into operation quickly at all the early fires.

First Stage (in and out of the district) of the regional scheme [whereby brigades were brought in from neighbouring areas; Stages Two and Three covered increasingly distant regions and were steadily more desperate] was operated at 19.40 — sixteen minutes after the first call. At this time all the fires were being controlled, but at 19.59 it was felt that the attack was developing on a large scale and Second Stage (in and out) was operated. By now, seventy-one calls had been received and all the local pumps were in action, and First Stage assistance was only just beginning to arrive. Thirty pumps from Third Stage and two turntable ladders were requested at 20.02, as it was now apparent that the raid was unusually heavy.[27]

Gas cut off

The Alert Warning was received in the control room at 19.10. Immediately bombs were heard to be falling, the district governor pressures were reduced from the normal four to four and a half inches to two inches, and that in the high pressure ring main from eight pounds per square inch to zero.

At 20.30, gas valves shut at both ends on the twenty-four inch connecting main between Folehill Gas Works and the Gas Street Works. An incendiary bomb had pierced the crown of the Gas Street holder, the gas had ignited and men were endeavouring to extinguish the flames. Another building at Gas Street was also on fire.

By 20.35, a heavy explosive bomb had demolished the mains fittings stores and five minutes later the gasholder outlet valve closed, thus shutting off completely gas supplies to the city. Barely half an hour after the raid had begun, at exactly 20.48, the:

Gasholder collapsed in flames, the crown and side sheets having been torn by blast. Later, the offices, garages and governor house were fired and, in the latter building, governors destroyed and serious damage done to valves and connections to trunk mains. The casualties at Gas Street were seven men killed and four injured. Of the latter, three received severe burns on the hands when the holder collapsed.[52]

The Alvis hit

I was on my round to Lamb Street where there were more shelters, when someone said, "The Alvis has been hit."......It was really ablaze — you couldn't do anything about it. You'd just got to leave it, but there were several people trying to do little bits with buckets and sand, which was hopeless. Their main job was to stop the fire spreading to the houses.

They said that the night shift had got out, that was at about 7.45, or a bit later, so I went back to the school shelters. That's where it got hit, and I was lucky to get out. I kept popping back to the works, but it was still ablaze.

*The remains of the main platform of the Coventry
railway station after the blitz*

24

Lord Dudley

I was entertaining the Home Secretary Mr Herbert Morrison, the Under Secretary of State Miss Ellen Wilkinson, the Military General of the local forces, my principal officer Captain Patterson, and many other people of importance in the region to dinner to discuss the question of placing all the fire brigades in the twenty-six local authorities which comprised the region into the control of the Regional Commissioner. I was suddenly told, in the middle of dinner, that a serious raid on Coventry had commenced and I sent my second principal officer, Mr Todd MP, hurrying up to report to me. As soon as he got there he telephoned to me (luckily before the telephone line was completely cut) to say that the raid was a very serious one indeed.

I left my dinner and went straight up to Coventry where I found Captain Hector, the Chief Constable, who was my Chief Regional Officer in Coventry and a man of exceptional ability, gallantry and good sense, and Mrs Pearl Hyde who was head of the WVS [Women's Voluntary Service] and one of the most remarkable women it has ever been my pleasure to know in life.

When I got there, the bombs were thundering down and although I was subjected to very many intense bombardments by German artillery in the First World War, I never experienced anything as severe as this one.

The city was a blaze of fire and I quickly discovered that the city fire brigade was nothing like as competent as it should have been for fighting these fires and I had to send for several fire brigades from Birmingham, Nuneaton, and other towns in the region to help fight the fires. [NB: According to the Chief Fire Officer, he had done this himself long before.] I at once found Captain Hector and Mrs Hyde and we went out to see what damage was taking place. The first thing that happened, to our terrible dismay as we were standing outside my headquarters which was next to the Cathedral, was a series of bombs falling and completely destroying the beautiful old Cathedral.

My Civil Defence workers were doing their utmost and I personally saw very many cases of people buried under debris being dug out by them. But the damage was terrific.[44]

The burning of the Cathedral

[About] seven o'clock the sirens wailed the alarm. The fire watchers and air raid wardens scurried to their posts up and down the city. The provost of Coventry Cathedral, the Very Reverend Richard Howard, lifted his tin hat from its peg and put it on as he dashed to the Cathedral, for there was no time to be lost. As he entered the dark, echoing building, a shadowy figure joined him. The dim light from the Provost's hand torch showed him it was Jock Forbes, a skilled stone mason, one of the Cathedral guard for fire watching.

"Full moon tonight, Jock," the Provost remarked.

"Aye, it's a raiders' moon right enough, Provost," Jock Forbes agreed. "When it's full up, it'll be like a spotlight over the city. I'm afraid we'll have trouble with that roof again tonight, sir."

"Yes, I fear it too," the Provost agreed, staring up above him, though his eye could not penetrate the gloom.

They were joined by two more watchers, Mr W H Eaton and Mr White, both younger men. These four men formed the Cathedral guard for the night. Away in the starry skies the droning began.

"It looks as if we shan't have long to wait," Mr Eaton said grimly as they took up their posts.

The Provost was worried about the roof of the Cathedral. It had been built five hundred years ago and, though it was a fine piece of workmanship, it had been made in such a way that modern fire bombs could lodge in it in unreachable places. The ceiling inside the Cathedral was flat, of beautiful oak panels which rested on huge beams that spanned the church. Above this inner ceiling, with a space of about eighteen inches between them, was an outer wooden roof supported on cross beams. The whole of it was covered by sheets of lead with their edges wrapped to each other round thin rollers of wood.

If a fire bomb managed to crash through the lead roof and come to rest on the inner ceiling, it was almost impossible to get at it in that narrow space. First, the lead had to be stripped back with crowbars to give the watchers room to work the stirrup pump on the flames. By the time this was done, the roof could be well alight. The fire watchers already had experience of this in a raid a month earlier when a fire-bomb had lodged in the space between roof and ceiling and started a fierce blaze which the stirrup pump could not reach. The fire brigade had arrived just in time and managed to put it out, but not before a certain amount of damage had been done.

The fire watchers made their way to the roof of the nave, the central portion of the Cathedral. The flat roof sparkled with frost in the moonlight.

"Ye'll need to watch your footing, Mr Howard," Jock Forbes warned the Provost. "These roofs will be slippery."

The drone of aircraft grew louder, throbbing, throbbing through the sky.

"There sounds like a lot of them tonight," Mr Eaton remarked.

The horrible beat of the enemy planes was almost overhead. A little to the north there was a sudden crash and almost at once flames leaped up into the darkness. Another crash, to the south this time, and another huge fire started. There was the heavier rumble of high explosive close at hand. Yet another fire sprang up, this time closer to the Cathedral.

"That looks like Owen Owen's store," someone remarked.

"They sound to be right overhead. It's time we took cover," the Provost decided. "We'd better step into the shelter of the spiral staircase." This was the place where they usually took cover during the worst of the raids. From the top of the spiral stone staircase that ran down from the roof of the nave to the north aisle, they could keep watch over a large part of the roof.

The smouldering ruins of St Michael's Cathedral shortly after the blitz

The whistle and crash of falling bombs came closer and closer. Soon the horizon to the north and west was ringed with a semi-circle of light.

"This is no ordinary tip and run raid, with a few bombers. This is going to be a bigger thing," Mr Forbes declared grimly.

It was all too plain that he was right. Soon there was a circle of fires around the centre of the city. Two of the watchers went to take up a position where they could see the roof of the south aisle.

Within the centre of the city an inferno reigned. There was the constant crash of high explosive; the roar and rumble of buildings collapsing; clouds of dust blotting out the stars; appalling flames suddenly leaping up as the fire-bombs fell and exploded; the hiss of water from many hoses; the shouts of the air raid wardens and firemen; the clatter of ambulances; the clang of fire engines. Within the Cathedral all was dark, silent and waiting. The watchers held their breath.

Then there was the sudden, fiendish whistle of falling bombs. Three fire-bombs struck the Cathedral at once. One fell on the roof of the Cathedral near the east end. Another plunged right through the roof and ceiling and fell among the pews at the head of the nave, and the third lodged in the roof of the south aisle, just above the organ. Instantly, the fire watchers sprang into action.

One of the younger men smothered with sand the bomb which had fallen on the chancel roof and, shovelling it up quickly, flung it over the battlemented wall into the Cathedral garden below, while another of the guards dashed to

27

tackle the one which had fallen through the roof to the floor of the nave. The bomb there was a large one and just beginning to blaze away among the oaken pews. Desperately, the fire watcher flung several buckets of sand over it before he could manage to extinguish it, shovel it into a scoop, and dash outside the Cathedral with it.

While all this was going on, the older fire watchers were tackling the bomb which had lodged between the roof and ceiling. Both of them were trying feverishly to rip the leaden sheets off the roof with crowbars. Above them was the never ceasing drone of enemy aircraft and the whine of falling bombs. Below them, in the cleft just above the organ, the bomb was blazing furiously on the oak ceiling. Once the ceiling gave way, the bomb would fall into the organ itself and there would be little hope of tackling it there. Heaving and hacking at the lead roof, so that they sweated heavily, even in the frosty air, the two men managed to make a hole big enough to pour in sand, but already the roof was blazing beyond the reach of the sand.

"We must get the fire brigade at once," the Provost decided, and passed word to the police to direct a fire brigade to the Cathedral.

"Aye, we'll get one right away, as soon as possible," the police officer promised and at once began to telephone the fire brigade headquarters.
The two younger fire watchers dashed to the roof to help with the spreading fire when they had dealt with their own bombs.

"This one will take all of us," Mr Forbes panted, as he worked the stirrup pump.

The four men worked feverishly, directing the jet of water to the fire, pumping frantically up and down, dashing up and down the ladders to bring buckets of water from the tap in the Smith's Chapel. The tap could just fill one bucket as fast as it could be used by the stirrup pump, so the guards had barely time to draw breath as they snatched up a bucket in turn from under the tap and placed another under it to be filling while they raced up to the roof with the full one.

Suddenly, there was a loud burst of high explosive as one of the men was going down the steep ladder to fetch water. The blast struck him and knocked him down. He fell to the bottom of the ladder and knocked his head against the masonry. The others heard the sound of his fall and came running to help him.

"Are you all right, man?" Jock called out from the top of the ladder as he saw a rather dazed figure rising to his feet again.

"Yes. I'm all right. The leather on my steel helmet took the shock." In another moment, the man was racing along with his bucket again.

All this time, the men had been working the stirrup pump and hacking back the lead sheets to let them get at the widely spreading flames. At last the fire was smothered out in the spray of stirrup pumps, but not before a large area of the roof had been burnt.

"Well, thank goodness that's out, but it took all four of us!" Mr Forbes gasped, dashing his arm across his brow to wipe away the perspiration. "If we get more than one at a time between the roof and the ceiling, it'll be more than we can manage without more help."

Hardly had he spoken, when another shower of fire-bombs fell and struck the roof of the Cappers' Chapel on the south side and passed through the leads and inside the ceiling and fell in a cascade of burning pieces. As the fire guards were already on the south side, they got to work at once with stirrup pumps and sand.

Through the clerestory windows one of them caught a glimpse of leaping flames on the roof of the north aisle.

"There's another bomb on the Smith's Chapel!" he exclaimed.

"I'll see to it," one of the younger men cried. "It's not gone through the leads yet."

Only one of them could be spared to deal with this new menace, for the rest were busy tackling the bombs inside the roof of the Cappers' Chapel. Water was running short, but they managed to extinguish the blaze. In a few minutes, the one who had gone to the Smith's Chapel returned.

"Luckily, the bomb had burst into fragments and the pieces hadn't gone through the roof," he explained. "I managed to put them out all right."

The fire guards were now panting for breath, perspiring profusely and almost exhausted. Beyond the Cathedral, the crash and roar of bombs was deafening and, from a hundred points in the city, flames soared upwards. Overhead, the drone of enemy planes went on and on. Hardly had the fire guard turned from one extinguished fire than there was another terrific rattle as a further shower of fire-bombs fell, four of them striking the roof of the Children's Chapel at the east end. They burst through the lead sheeting and lodged on the oaken beams, exploding into flames, and soon the roof there was a raging fire. The four men dashed round the building towards it. Through the holes they poured sand and water, but the fire grew fiercer as it spread.

"We've nearly used all the sand," one of the men gasped as he humped a sandbag up the ladder. "Only one or two more bags left now."

"We'll have to rely on water then," another man said, working the stirrup pump feverishly up and down. "If only the fire brigade would come!"

"The fire's gaining on us!" Jock Forbes exclaimed in despair as he redoubled his efforts to smother it out with the water jet.

"The spiral staircase is filled with smoke. We'll have to use the outside ladders now," one of the younger ones reported, coughing as he staggered up with a bucket. This meant a longer, more difficult journey to get water. The flames began to gain even a stronger hold. Though they still fought hard, the strength of the fire guards was becoming weaker with exhaustion in the face of the great heat from the flames. Four men could no longer keep those spreading fires in check. The ceiling was well ablaze.

Thick smoke drifted down into the Cathedral, to the Smith's Chapel where the water tap was. One of the younger men, undaunted, went in to fill his

The ruins of the Cathedral a few days after the raid

bucket again, but came out choking and groping for the entrance. Overcome
by the smoke, he had to be assisted by one of the others. It was impossible to
enter the Smith's Chapel again, so now the faithful fire watchers could get no
more water to fill their buckets. There was nothing they could do now to
extinguish the blazing roof, but hope and pray that the fire brigade would
reach them in time to save the rest of the Cathedral.

Worn out as they were, they still set about saving what treasures they could
from the east end of the Cathedral, the cross and candlesticks, the silver plate
and chalice and anything else they could manage to carry out before the fire
should spread to the roof at the end of the church. Streaming with perspiration
they worked till the smoke and fumes drove them back. Then they went to the
south porch to wait for the fire brigade to come.[49]

So started that moonlit night after which Goebbels was able to coin a new
term — to Coventrate. The sheer concentration of bombs tossed everyone
off balance. Emergency services were thrown into chaos because of burst
water mains, fractured gas pipes, destroyed telephone lines, roads impassable because of bomb craters and rubble, and a desperate sense of stunned
hopelessness as precious buildings, loved ones, and homes were blitzed
into ruins.

Autumn Prelude

Over the summer of 1940, Coventry had been subjected to an escalation of raids and warnings, from the first *warning* (bombs were dropped on Ansty aerodrome on 25 June) and the first *raid* (two days later when bombs were dropped on Hillfields, though some reports state that the first bombs to fall on the city were on 18 August at Canley), to far more regular, systematic, and heavier attention. These increased steadily during that Autumn.

By comparison with the coastal ports, Coventry escaped the early part of the War without substantial damage or loss of life. The first air raid to directly concern Coventry occurred on 25 June 1940, when five bombs were dropped on Ansty Aerodrome, a few miles to the east of the city. Two days later, sixteen people were killed during an air raid on the Hillfields area of the city. Between 25 August and 31 October 1940, Coventry was attacked on seventeen occasions, resulting in a large number of casualties: 176 dead, 229 seriously injured, and 451 slightly injured. [These figures are slightly less than those reported by the Chief Medical Officer, for a period a few days shorter].

During November 1940, the air raids on Coventry increased in both frequency and severity. Between 1 and 12 November there were seven air raids on Coventry, affecting nearly every part of the city. However, there was only one air raid which resulted in the loss of life or serious injury, the remainder causing damage or minor injuries only......

The number of casualties may have seemed bad enough at the time, but the EMS [Emergency Medical Services], barring a few minor problems, managed to cope with the situation. However, during the Coventry blitz, even the most well prepared and practised plans ended in chaos and confusion.[119]

Diary of Mary Bloomfield
(excerpts)

June 1940: Dunkirk. News began to filter through of the retreat and evacuation and we all became very apprehensive. Ken Jones from Dulverton Avenue was involved, as was Leslie Hartley next door. I cannot describe my relief when we had returned from town with our motorbike and sidecar and

31

we saw a very dirty, dishevelled Ken wearily going into his own gate. I ran across and spoke to him. "Oh, Ken, how glad I am that you are safe. I wouldn't have dared to speak to your mother if you hadn't come home."

Leslie also came home, but not [–]. He was taken prisoner of war whilst hiding in a sand dune, but it was some months before Doris had this confirmed. She decided to close up house and go to live with her mother in Eagle Street, Foleshill......

Monday 12 August 1940:   Went to the Plaza to see *Ninotchka* . During the newsreel a woman sitting behind me suddenly said, "Oh, God, shall we ever come out of this nightmare?", but that is not the general opinion. We know that we must win or perish. Sixty German planes were shot down over the Channel yesterday.

Tuesday 17 September: A strong gale is blowing for which we must be thankful. Flat bottom barges which the Germans plan to use to invade us are useless in heavy seas.

Last night a German bomber ran into the balloon barrage. The crew, knowing that they must crash, dropped their bombs at random and baled out. The bombs fell in Wallace Road, Radford, causing the worst damage to Coventry so far. There are about twenty dead. One bomb fell near to an Anderson shelter and blew it to bits. Seven people inside were killed and the house completely demolished. The bomber crashed in flames at Walsgrave. Three of the crew died when their parachutes failed to open and the fourth broke a leg. The balloon came down in the centre of the city, in Broadgate.[22]

From the *Midland Daily Telegraph* war diary

10 May 1940:   The invasion of Belgium, Holland and Luxembourg at 3 am produced a profound effect on the people of Coventry and district. For the first time since the outbreak of war nine months before, it seemed that the war was starting in earnest. Every effort was made to overhaul ARP arrangements and all military leave was stopped.

25 June 1940:   Coventry had its first real air raid alarm when sirens sounded at 12.42 am on this morning. All ARP posts and AFS [Auxiliary Fire Service] state that action stations were fully manned, while searchlights traced the sky. At Pailton, eleven bombs were dropped in and near the village, rendering five families homeless and other houses temporarily uninhabitable. Five bombs were also dropped in the vicinity of Ansty Aerodrome.

18 August 1940:   Coventry had its first actual air raid shortly after mid-night. No sirens were sounded, but everyone was wakened by the dropping of fourteen high explosive bombs in Canley Road and Cannon Hill Road.

25 August 1940:   Hundreds of bombs were dropped from 9.15 pm on Sunday 25 August to 5 am the next day. The Rex Cinema in Corporation Street was completely wrecked and a number of houses very badly damaged and fires started at many points. Rootes N° 2 Shadow Factory at Ryton was made a target of incendiary bombs. One dropped on the factory, but was extinguished by works firemen before it committed damage. Others caused a big fire in the dump of the contractor building the factory.

August 1940:   During this month and September countless wild rumours gained currency in the Coventry district about men alleged to have been signalling to enemy aircraft being shot dead by Home Guards. The only foundation at the time of writing was that there was considerable activity on the part of the Home Guard, military and police to track down possible fifth columnists believed to be shining lights for the guidance of aircraft.

September 1940:   Coventry had its first experience of a daylight dive bombing raid. Shortly before 5.30 and a few minutes after the sounding of the sirens, the raider appeared out of the clouds and, with unerring accuracy, made for what was, presumably, its target, the Standard Motor works at Canley. He scored a direct hit with a heavy calibre high explosive bomb and two large, oil-type incendiary bombs, and big fires started. Damage in the Paint Shop was considerable, although not of prime war importance. Eye witnesses were full of praise for the superb airmanship of the raider's pilot as he made his way through the balloon barrage, banking steeply more than once to avoid, not only the cables, but also fire from ground defences which opened up before he was more than half way across the city.[93]

First encounters with war

I'd just been married in February [1940] and the first encounter I had was walking along Corporation Street one Saturday morning when a German plane came over and machinegunned us.

   The second thing that I remember vividly is the Rex Cinema in Corporation Street which one Sunday night went with the wind. The film *Gone With The Wind* was due to start on the Monday, but that Sunday night that went, and Hogarths, and a few more little shops.[111]

My earliest recollection was a bright, red glow in the sky from my bedroom window.

   "Are you frightened?" whispered my brother.

   No, I just couldn't understand the sun rising so late at night.

   Next morning, we discovered it was an RAF plane that had crashed onto the cricket pitch at the back of the Bulls Head. Just a mass of twisted metal, burnt beyond recognition, with one wheel sticking up like a toffee apple. Did he crash onto the cricket pitch to avoid the houses? It was a dark night, how could he have seen it?

The next plane I saw crash was also RAF. Brought down by a barrage balloon operated by WAAFs [Women's Auxiliary Air Force] on the common at the top of our road. I watched it fall, twisting round like a sycamore pod, till it finally disappeared behind the houses. The local fire engine was on the scene within minutes; I followed behind on my bike and arrived in time to watch them carry away the pilot's body covered by a blanket. The plane crashed on allotments surrounded by houses: another miracle.

Underground shelters were built in Primrose Hill Park. I spent many a long night in those shelters, listening to bombs dropping and an old man playing the accordion.

My mother took my younger brother and me to Evesham, to escape the bombing. Dad stayed behind, working in the Daimler factory.[9]

The first time the sirens went we were all frightened to death because we had been warned about the night raids. We all ran down the shelter in our night dresses, so there wasn't a pair of you-know-whats between any of the women. It was terrible. We were all so frightened, but it was laughable. It caused quite a bit of fun.[84]

The Hillfields district of Coventry seemed to be a regular target, but, with the Ordnance factory and the Rover works being merely the biggest of the local workshops, plumb in the middle of a thickly populated area, it was to be expected that people living there would suffer.

Homeward bound one September afternoon, there was a distant explosion somewhere behind me. I pulled into the kerb, turned, scanned the sky, saw nothing. Later, I heard that a hit and run raider had dropped its load onto the paint shop of the Standard Motor works at Canley. Some weeks later the German propagandists boasted of that success and named Chief Pilot Storp as the bomber's captain. But it was remarkable that a daylight intruder could penetrate the heart of England without being intercepted on the way in; it seemed ominous.[98]

The night the first bomb fell on Coventry [she is, in fact remembering a raid in October 1940] was quite an experience. It was a source of irritation that during an air raid Alert a number of men were standing smoking outside the shelter with their glowing cigarettes. Thus, when the high scream note of the bomb was heard there was a dash down the steps of the shelter. The ground shook beneath our feet as the bomb fell on the nearby Daimler factory, and was followed by two more further away.

On the way to work at the London Road laundry the following morning I passed through Eagle Street, where all the houses had been damaged by the second bomb, the third bomb having fallen on Harnall Lane.[79]

Night after night, or so it seemed, we trudged down the garden path in pitch darkness to the Anderson shelter at the bottom of the garden. Lots of voices could be heard, presumably neighbours going to their shelters or to the communal shelter further down our street.

Shouts of "Put out that light!" or, "This way!" or, "Where are you?" punctuated the night air as everyone scampered about in pyjamas and overcoats whilst the distant sirens wailed. Then we were in the shelter, with its inevitable damp and fusty smell. An old Valor paraffin stove provided both light and heat in our shelter and there was a good supply of blankets. I don't ever remember going to sleep. We just sat or lay there listening to the unmistakable throbbing sound of the German bombers mingled with distant explosions and gunfire.

One explosion was not quite so distant, however, and the whistling of that particular bomb will remain with me forever. My father said afterwards that he was convinced that it had our name on it — it seemed directly overhead. As soon as they heard it, my parents acted instantly. Dad turned the Valor stove off and threw himself on top of me after Mum had thrown a blanket over my head. The explosion was deafening but we were still in one piece. The bomb had landed about eighty yards away on the edge of a field.[11]

When we were off duty at 6 pm [from the GPO in Hertford Street], I used to cycle home hell for leather down the Binley Road to get home before the sirens went......

When we did a split duty, off at 1 pm and back at 5 pm, I often used to go to the Empire with my mother, who brought me sandwiches and a flask of tea. As we then worked from 5 pm to 8 pm, often the siren went and, apart from a few left on duty, we went down to the shelter in Greyfriars Lane, if we could get in. It was such a good shelter that postmasters from various post offices in town, Gosford Street, etc, used to be already there. On the night of the heavy raid on Liverpool, eight of us took our chances on the floor of the Main Post Office; luckily, no stray bombs came down.[86]

I can still make out the faded S for Shelter in what is remaining of Lower Spon Street, where we made our way to go underground, below the old Rudge works and, after a very bad raid, the streets running with water from damaged mains, hoses criss-crossing all over like a great snakes and ladders board. The red glow of burning buildings, several bodies covered by blankets against a wall.

I remember us kids sent down the far end when a lady was carried in and laid on one of the wooden bunks. I now realise she was in labour. The police and ARP wardens and a sailor made a screen around her, facing us. I heard her screaming and crying, then there was a baby crying. I asked my mum about it and she told me to be quiet.[76]

In August 1940, aged eleven and just discharged from hospital severely disabled by polio, I moved with my parents, brother Bill, thirteen, and sister Valerie, nine, to the Ivy Cottage, a pub in King William Street, Hillfields. Within days there were isolated daylight raids made by lone bombers......

Over those two or three months leading up to the 14 November raid, the nearest building to our pub in every direction was hit by something. Apart from the three houses immediately behind in Albert Street, that were destroyed, taking our back entry with them, the shop immediately opposite us was burned to the ground. A small lemonade bottling factory next door on one side was, I think, twice set alight, and the Palladium, next door on the other, had two seats burnt by incendiaries. Despite all this, and incendiaries on the pub which failed to set fire to us, the pub never closed.[91]

Shortages and queues

Ration books, clothing coupons, queues at the shops when something extra was in, my mother trying to make the rations stretch, myself putting gravy browning on my legs to look like stockings when my coupons wouldn't stretch to a new pair. (Couldn't do that on a wet day, though.) Carrying a gas mask everywhere.

I worked at Bushills in Little Park Street in those days and I remember the times we had to race down several flights of stairs to the basement air raid shelter whenever the air raid warning went. At times, we'd just reached the shelter when the All Clear went and we had to trek back up again.[77]

It was a time of discomfort, of eternally crowded trains and bare Nissen huts, of blackouts and the drab vigils of sentry-go. It was a time of exhortation, admonition, repetition, when the eye was everywhere confronted with security posters and aircraft recognition silhouettes, and PAD notices and fire orders. It was a time of weekly respirator drill, of Wings for Victory and warship weeks, of training films (Was there a soldier anywhere in Britain who did not see *Next of Kin*.......?)[40]

It was also a time of being constantly confronted with security posters warning that walls have ears, against careless whispers, urging people to dig for victory, to be on their guard, to be vigilant. Films of the time, often propaganda based, Pathé News, newspapers promoting the war effort, soldiers, trucks and military equipment everywhere, all added to the tension and growing awareness of the impact the War was starting to have.

Workers billetted

With the outbreak of war, thousands of workers were moved to Coventry to work in the war factories. Billetting officers went around assessing people's spare rooms and forcing them to take in workers. Nearby towns such as Leamington Spa did not escape and had to take their quota as well:

After the local factories geared up for production of armoured vehicles, jeeps, planes, etc, workers had to be brought in from other areas, so we constantly had officials knocking our doors enquiring how many rooms were in the house and how many residents. I had a single bed in my spare room, so a young girl from Tyneside came to stay with us and remained happily for three years.[10]

Home Guard drill

Every Sunday morning, Dad's Home Guard battalion would march past the top of the street ("There's my Dad!"), presumably on the way to exercise in the fields around Allesley......
One day, on the way home from school, we saw an aeroplane flying very low and had just identified it as German when we heard the rat-tat-tat of gunfire, apparently coming from the plane. Within seconds we were hustled into houses, but the fun was all over by then.
Shopping in the city centre usually meant standing in endless queues outside shops whose windows had been boarded up. I remember particularly a biscuit shop at the end of the arcade leading to the Barras Market. The biscuits always seemed to be the same kind. We frequently called at the food office at the bottom of Hertford Street, presumably to get new ration books, and what a cheerless building that was......[83]

Barrage balloons on the loose!

Another thing I shall never forget was the almost total darkness in our street at night owing to the street lights being off. And then there were the searchlights probing the sky, sometimes just practising, and the barrage balloons. We often went to have a look at the balloon site just off Kingsbury Road. The balloon looked quite comical when it was on the ground and flopping about like a drunken elephant.[83]

The barrage balloon in the park broke loose from its moorings one night and dragged its chains all across our chimney pots. We thought it was another bomb! I flew down two flights of stairs into the shelter in the basement and when I came out, all the soot had come down the chimney and absolutely covered the room. On getting ready for bed again (my husband worked on nightshift), looking out of the window in the dark, I suddenly saw a plane on fire, seemingly coming straight for me. I flew down to the shelter again. I heard later a German plane had been shot down and crashed at Wyken.[126]

UXB

We, Joe and I, were married in the early part of the war and after only sixteen weeks in our own home Joe was called up to the Air Force. I waved him off and returned to live at home. My Dad built an Anderson shelter with good bunk beds in, where we slept. I did, anyway. I'd rather have stopped in bed, but Dad wouldn't allow that.

When there were raids, Dad would pop in the house to fetch jugs of cocoa when it went a bit quiet. One evening after tea, I'd gone upstairs to put long trousers on, ready for fire fighting, when there was this mighty thump and the house shook (semi-detached) and Mother shouted a great deal for me to hurry up. Later, we discovered it was a land UXB [Unexploded bomb] three doors away, so quite a lot of us had to evacuate for a few days. We stayed with my eldest brother and family. Mother couldn't settle and it was agony to see people walking with their possessions in prams and on bicycles along the main road to the outskirts of the city. After a while we also went into the country, to relations, where it didn't seem as if there was a war on, except for all the forces knitting that was done. On the 14 November 1940 we returned for a few days. I went to post a letter before 7 pm, just a short walk, and never arrived home till about 8 am on the fifteenth, because of that unforgettable night.[61]

"It all depends on me, and I depend on God"

Blackout, bombs, shortages, rationing, queues, separations, long working hours, comradeship, tears and laughter, and the motto on Holy Trinity church:

"IT ALL DEPENDS ON ME AND I DEPEND ON GOD"

I used to muse about that as I stood waiting for the Nº 21 bus which started in

Trinity Street from outside the ruins of the old Owen Owen store. The buses finished running at 9 pm, so it was Shank's pony after an evening in the town, at the pictures or a dance, and many is the time I walked home alone late at night with no fear of being robbed.

I should have mentioned honesty as another memory. There were no private cars on the road, except doctors and maybe ARP wardens. Petrol was rationed and only people with certain qualifications were allowed a petrol ration. All cars were laid up for the duration but, as very few of the ordinary folk possessed a car, that aspect of wartime did not bother most people.

Everyone had to be registered for a ration book and the population between the ages of eighteen and forty-five was liable for call-up, either for the forces or essential work. Women who had young children were exempt. I came within this age group and was working at Courtaulds when war broke out. Things went fairly normally for a few months as we finished off the work that was on order and of course there was a demand for nylon for parachutes and other material for uniforms, so we were kept busy for some time in the textile trade.

Owing to the blackout we started to work daylight shifts and cut short our lunchtimes and worked on Saturday afternoons during the winter to get as many hours daylight as possible.[80]

Mothers and children evacuated

I lived in Edgwick Road......in premises with top shop weaving businesses above. I can remember being down our Anderson shelter on my own with my new baby. In those days we had to pack another lot of clothes ready, for sometimes it was an all-night session in the shelter. I wonder if anyone remembers the old Coventry Post Office on Stoney Stanton Road, which was only a hundred yards from my shelter? It received a complete direct hit with a bomb and all around was a shambles. What a blessing the shelters were, although it was creepy, hearing bombs whistling down.

Then the memories of us mums-to-be. We were all evacuated. We had to be at the Council House, then we were put in cars, our husbands didn't know where [we were going] to until they heard from us. Some went to Leamington or Warwick. Me, I was unloaded at Shipston-on-Stour. Some lady with a mansion let us have a wing of her property. We had to clean and do chores, so she got free servants.

The Maternity Hospital was not far away. Can you imagine us every night, crowded round the attic windows, sobbing our socks off, looking at the bright red sky, knowing our city was being bombed.

No fine cribs for our babies when they were born, just boxes. My friend's baby got suffocated in one, so we were all anxious.[80]

Because there were a lot of London children there [in Deddington, where she had been evacuated], there was not enough room, so some days I went to school in the British Legion club room upstairs, and sometimes at a private house in Deddington.

I remember we had sticking plaster criss-crossed over all the windows in case of blast. And the blackout curtains. Everyone who went out of the door had to switch the lights out first. If you didn't, somebody would shout, "Put that light out!" or the Air Raid Warden would come knocking at your door.

We all had to carry gas masks. They were all in square boxes at first and then we all had quite trendy cases. I remember my young baby brother had a gas mask. We had to lie him down inside, tie it around his waist and keep pumping. I am glad we didn't need them. I didn't like the ones for the babies.[26]

Harsh working conditions

The war effort of the men at Ribble Road and Red Lane will always be associated with the physical conditions in which they worked, conditions which were aggravated, if not entirely caused, by the blackout regulations. These were much more stringent than in the First World War, but reminders of the need for them did not relieve the irritation. In place of corrugated iron sheets in the stamp shops, walls of brick were built half way up the inside structure, and at the entrances to each shop there was a light trap with double entrances, so that none of the lurid glare of the furnaces could penetrate the outside darkness. The men operating the hammers were confined within great compartments to which cooling air had no inlet, and they worked in the midst of heat, smoke and dust, with a fortitude that won the admiration of all who witnessed the scenes of their labours.

Many other preparations had been made. The works had been camouflaged as effectively as possible from aircraft. Deep shelters had been built and official orders were strict on the need for men to stop work during periods of danger and go down into the shelters. There was a volunteer fire brigade; there was a body of Local Defence Volunteers, the name of which was changed to the Home Guard; air raid precautions came under the supervision of a special unit; and a team had been trained in first aid……

A night shift had begun at Ribble Road after the spurious concordat of Munich, and now, when the production of war material was being accelerated, the great difficulty was to find sufficient workmen. There were seven hundred and fifty on the pay-roll, but for full efficiency many more were needed. Under a scheme sponsored by the Government, men were brought in from other industrial districts. The personnel officer went to Swansea to enlist tinplate workers, for whom there was no employment in that area, and the main advantage of drafting in these particular men was that they were accustomed to working in conditions of great heat. Because of this, stamping firms had priority over all others in the enlistment of these tinplate men. Women were enrolled as well, and a large draft came from Brighton. Most of these had been waitresses in hotels and had never in their lives seen a place like a drop-forging works; nor had they ever heard any noise quite like the thunder of the great hammers; but they proved to be quick and adaptable, and carried out their duties with splendid resolution.[96]

Cash's at Kingfield

During this period there were a number of daytime alerts, not only in London and Southern England, but also in the Midlands. For a time, the wailing of the sirens during working hours caused some considerable dislocation to activities at Kingfield, owing to all employees having to take shelter. Although this was carried out smoothly and with good organisation, the periods of the Alerts were of sufficient duration to cause an appreciable loss of working hours. Fortunately, we had an excellent system of concrete covered trenches which had been constructed on the sports ground prior to the outbreak of war. These were capable of accommodating all our employees. At night they were used by our own tenants and others in the neighbourhood.

During October 1940, there were few nights without a siren, the moonlight periods being particularly favourable to the enemy. Life for the citizens of Coventry became very trying; many people slept, or tried to sleep, every night in air raid shelters, which generally entailed sitting on a closely packed bench and securing such fitful sleep as was possible. It was hardly to be expected that people would be in good shape for a day's work after nights passed under such conditions.

A considerable number of bombs fell on Coventry during this month, causing damage and casualties, although not on a great scale......[6]

Raids were so numerous that autumn, when my husband was away working, that getting ready for the nightly ordeal was a ritual for thousands. I used to take baby underground in the clothes basket, with blankets, food and drinks to last the night. [51]

Evacuating nightly

......there were people, of course, who were moving away at night time......evacuating nightly, going out into the country, coming back home to do their jobs of work......[66]

......there were many who felt safer leaving the city each night for places like Corley Rocks and Whitley Common......[74]

Everyone who could, got out to the country, on buses or trams, or whatever was available. They went loaded with things that really meant something to them. Some took blankets, food and so forth, but some only took their money and insurance papers. But when we went, we took lolly for a drink, which we had in the Craven Arms, Binley, when it was available. That wasn't very often, as most pubs only opened for about two hours for drinking, but they couldn't close, even when the beer went off. Some folks who didn't go down the shelters stayed for the company, talking and having a sing-song to keep their minds off what was going on. But not for long.

We went into the Craven and met a fellow who said he couldn't take us home with him that night until he had talked it over with his wife (or until they had discussed how much to charge us, more like). We found out later this was what a lot of the families were doing. How much they could rook out of folks who only wanted a good night's sleep. Anyhow, this chap said we would be safe on top of Binley pit, so off we went, him showing us the way. He told us to go into one of the tunnels that the trucks ran through and he went home. It was bitterly cold. My Mum, Tom and I couldn't sleep so at 1.30 am we woke up my Dad and said we would be warmer walking home and he agreed. Off we went. It seemed an endless trudge......

One night (when, is not clear from Mrs Harris' account), she was in the Ivy Cottage in Hillfields:

One night we were in there and it started raining incendiaries and small bombs were dropped on Hillfields and other parts of the city......King William Street was alight like Blackpool illuminations and a string of trams were all down the street. They couldn't move them and a water main had been hit outside The Clock pub, as folks often called it......some fellow passed this water main...... he got a little too near and it shot him up into the air, just like those balls you shoot at at the fair. Well, when they came back and told us, we could see the funny side of it and we laughed till the tears rolled down our faces.[60]

Raids build up ominously

I was in the AFS works fire brigade and really enjoyed it. There used to be six girls and six men on duty at night — but not in the same hut! We went to work in the morning to do a day's work (I was in the toolroom at this time, drilling, milling, filing; anything that wanted doing we did, me and Bett), then we went to the canteen for tea, then back on duty.

Sometimes we managed to have a short sleep in turns, but if we had a mauve [purple] light come on, we knew the planes had just come over the coast and then, when we saw the red light come on, they were overhead — no sleep then!

6.30 am and over to the canteen for breakfast — fat bacon or kippers, not much of a choice — then straight into work for another day's slog. And when I hear kids today say, when they get home at 4.15 pm, "I'm shattered, I've been up since 6.30 am," I wonder how they would have stood up to it in those days, working straight through twenty-four hours and we couldn't take a day off. If we did, we were reported to a tribunal.[60]

Through September and October night raids began, gradually building up in scale, frequency and intensity. Hillfields, with much industry set in working class streets, was hard hit in this period, more so than on the night of 14/15 November.

Eventually, after initially yo-yoing up and down to the beer cellar [of the Ivy Cottage] in response to every Alert and All Clear, we children and our mother spent every night down there, on mattresses and two camp beds of my father's from the Great War amongst and on top of the beer barrels. My father insisted on sleeping upstairs.

From early on the manager of the Palladium Cinema next door stayed most nights with us and later, during severe raids, we had up to thirty customers down there, frightened to risk the hazards of the streets.

The bars tended to be packed at that time and years later my mother used to say that publicans in the South had no conception of the number of barrels of beer we got through in a week. If people weren't able to *forget* in drink, they were, perhaps, able to dull their senses.

One night some Irishmen lodging in a house in Albert Street directly behind us had become 'difficult', refusing to drink up. Eventually, twenty minutes after closing time, my father had to eject them. Ten minutes later, he was leading the search party trying to dig them out of the wreckage of their home. He stayed there till 3 am. I can still remember the enormous bang of the cellar door slamming, followed by the cloud of dust as the bomb struck. From then on I *was* frightened.[91]

Bombed buildings in the shadow of Holy Trinity church

We had been the target of enemy bombers for about three months prior to the November blitz, Birmingham and Coventry sharing the attentions of the Luftwaffe on alternate nights for weeks. We in Coventry would see the glow of fires on the skyline and know that it was Brum's turn, and we would speculate as to how the citizens were faring. The following evening it would be our turn.

The sirens would sound about 7 pm (we almost set our clocks by "Wailing Winnie") and soon the drone of plane engines would be heard, followed by the crump, crump of exploding bombs. We had no deep shelters, people took cover wherever they could. Under the stairs or the table were popular spots.

At this time I was employed at Courtaulds. One morning, when reaching the factory gates, all employees were sent home because, following the previous night's raid, a hole had been found in the sports field which was thought to be a delayed action bomb. There would be danger to the workers if it exploded, as we had glass roofs. Reporting back to work the next day, we learned that our 'delayed action' was merely the hole left by the flagpole when it was blown out of the ground. This caused much leg pulling from other nearby factory employees.

One of my workmates had her entire family killed by enemy action and there were many more similar tragedies throughout the city during October.

Anderson shelters were being issued, neighbours having to share the use of them as supplies were not enough to enable each house to be provided with one.

During this period Coventrians got a bit superstitious about the film *Gone with the Wind* , which was due for showing at our newest cinema, the Rex. But the building was totally destroyed by a direct hit the night before the first showing. Luckily, there were no casualties. A few weeks later, the film was to be shown at the Savoy, but once again, the building had "gone with the wind".[58]

October — countdown to blitzkrieg

This excerpt from the log of air raid Warnings and All Clears from the air raid precaution unit at the Daimler shows the build-up of the raids clearly. Many were for planes passing over to other cities and back again, but observe the ominous regularity of the evening Alerts, steadily moving earlier, from 8.30 to 7.30 in October and 7.30 to 7.05 in November, as the nights drew in. The 'dates' clearly include, in some cases, overnight shifts.

Warnings and All Clears

Date	Alert	All Clear
7 October 1940	08.12 pm	10.27 pm
"	01.17 am	01.35 am
"	01.51 am	02.14 am
8 October 1940	09.45 am	10.04 am
"	02.22 pm	02.58 pm
"	08.20 pm	10.00 pm
"	11.19 pm	11.44 pm
"	04.45 am	05.07 am
9 October 1940	07.18 pm	07.32 pm
"	02.57 am	03.15 am
"	03.39 am	04.09 am
10 October 1940	11.21 pm	11.37 pm
"	01.23 am	01.54 am
"	02.49 am	03.28 am
12 October 1940	08.40 pm	11.01 pm
(25 IBs [Incendiary bombs] dropped on works, causing fires)		
13 October 1940	02.15 pm	02.36 pm
"	07.55 pm	08.02 pm
"	08.39 pm	09.19 pm
"	09.47 pm	10.53 pm

13 October 1940	12.19 am	02.47 am
14 October 1940	07.14 pm	07.41 pm
"	08.08 pm	01.35 am

(4 HEs [High explosives] dropped on works)

15 October 1940	01.36 am	02.13 am
"	08.10 pm	04.05 am
16 October 1940	08.06 pm	09.33 pm
"	10.05 pm	04.04 pm
17 October 1940	03.38 pm	04.40 pm
"	07.57 pm	10.22 pm
18 October 1940	08.25 pm	11.27 pm
19 October 1940	12.17 pm	12.29 pm
"	07.42 pm	10.15 pm
"	10.29 pm	11.10 pm
20 October 1940	01.47 pm	02.04 pm
"	07.39 pm	05.45 am
21 October 1940	10.10 am	10.27 am
"	10.47 am	11.06 am
"	11.51 am	12.42 pm
"	07.41 pm	12.12 am
22 October 1940	11.17 am	12.04 pm
"	07.43 pm	10.25 pm

(3 HEs dropped on works)

24 October 1940	12.09 pm	12.29 pm
"	07.50 pm	11.12 pm
25 October 1940	07.52 pm	11.12 pm
"	11.34 pm	12.12 am
26 October 1940	07.07 pm	12.14 am
27 October 1940	06.43 pm	06.54 pm
"	07.43 pm	02.31 am
"	06.19 am	06.51 am
28 October 1940	11.34 am	11.54 am
"	07.38 pm	11.22 pm
"	06.15 am	06 28 am
29 October 1940	07.54 pm	01.38 am
"	02.57 am	04.52 am
30 October 1940	11.43 am	12.20 pm
"	07.43 pm	09.59 pm
31 October 1940	01.40 pm	03.32 pm
"	03.47 pm	04.49 pm
"	03.05 am	03.29 am
"	04.05 am	05.15 am
1 November 1940	01.39 pm	01.49 pm
"	07.28 pm	09.30 pm

1 November 1940	10.09 pm	11.50 pm
2 November 1940	06.55 am	07.35 am
3 November 1940	03.45 pm	04.56 pm
4 November 1940	01.17 pm	02.08 pm
"	07.51 pm	09.25 pm
"	12.41 am	02.24 am
"	04.41 am	04.51 am
5 November 1940	06.49 pm	07.36 pm
"	03.57 am	04.45 am
6 November 1940	06.40 pm	06.51 pm
"	07.21 pm	07.31 pm
"	10.45 pm	12.05 am
[7 November 1940]	07.36 pm	09.09 pm
"	10.35 pm	11.07 pm
"	11.58 pm	12.45 am
8 November 1940	08.21 am	08.37 am
"	12.35 pm	12.53 pm
"	07.05 pm	11.35 pm
"	02.05 am	02.32 am
9 November 1940	12.01 pm	01.11 pm
"	03.17 pm	04.07 pm
"	05.03 pm	05.18 pm
"	07.05 pm	08.33 pm
10 November 1940	07.05 pm	10.00 pm
"	10.33 pm	11.44 pm
"	02.34 am	02.51 am
11 November 1940	11.59 am	12.26 pm
"	03.11 pm	03.53 pm
12 November 1940	07.36 pm	08.12 pm
"	09.09 pm	11.48 pm
"	12.20 am	12.35 am
13 November 1940	12.44 pm	02.23 pm
"	03.54 pm	04.49 pm
"	06.41 pm	06.53 pm
14 November 1940	09.45 am	10.15 am
"	07.09 pm	06.20 am

(First blitz)

Air raid damage to parent factory

26 August 1940:   Two bombs — one in sports field and one on railway siding near shadow factory. Both HE. No material damage to this factory.

12 October 1940:   Incendiary bomb attack. Fires in Aero offices and Main Stores. Daimler brigade and fire watchers operated and no help required. No serious casualties. Traces of twenty-six IBs found on the following morning.

14 October 1940:   Incendiary and HE bomb attack. One string of HEs across the factory. First landed in the road by Gas Meter House, Daimler Road, setting fire to the gas main.
Second on Main Drive, by Experimental Shop.
Third on Boulton Paul Shop.
Fourth on Polishing Shop.
All fires, including the gas main, dealt with without outside help, and no major casualties, but considerable damage to shops and buildings.

22 October 1940:   HE attack, no fires.
One bomb on Spare Parts Dept.
One bomb on Paint Shop.
One bomb on railway siding by Cleansing Station.
Damage considerable to Spare Parts Dept and Paint Shop.[5]

Diary of Mary Bloomfield
(extracts)

Saturday 5 October [1940]:   We have had till now a lull in the air raids on Coventry. Birmingham gets them regularly and we get used to hearing the planes going over there. We get the sirens day and night, but don't take much notice of them.

Sunday 6 October: Last night we had the first really bad air raid on Coventry. It lasted continuously from 8.30 pm to 10.30 pm. It started very suddenly, before the sirens went. The first thing I heard was a bomb dropping and then the gun-fire. I collected my things and dashed for shelter. The Johnsons came in with Barry. The gun-fire hardly stopped at all and, as it was the first raid of any consequence, we thought lots of shells were bombs.
Ted was on 2 pm to 10 pm, changing to early duty. He managed to slip round to see us. There were about 180 HE bombs and 600 incendiaries. Allesley was alight with them. The first bomb hit the arcade in Smithford Street. Several shops in Smithford Street and Queen Victoria Road, also in Gosford Street, were on fire. No military targets were hit but there were some very near shots. We got the All Clear about 10.30 pm, but it was 3 am before Ted came home. He couldn't go back on duty until 8 am. Two policemen were killed at the top of Bishop Street when a bomb fell on The Grapes public house.

Monday 7 October: Last night was quiet here. We went to bed and slept in, despite guns going off in Birmingham.

Tuesday 8 October: I did Mrs Burdett's hair yesterday afternoon — Ted was late coming home because of a siren Alert. We had the sirens at 8 pm, but had time to get to the shelter before the guns started firing. Bombs fell all over the town again and there were big fires. Again, nothing of importance was hit, although several bombs were very close to important targets. The Motor Mart on London Road was burnt out. The nearby cemetery wall was hit, but most damage was confined to streets and private dwellings. It didn't seem quite as bad as Saturday because there were lulls between the relays of enemy aircraft coming in, but it lasted longer. Ted had to sleep in the shelter. He had the top bunk, Ken Johnson had the bottom one. Mrs Johnson and I shared one of the seats and we made up a bed for Barry on the other one. The All Clear went about 3 am, so we all went to our houses to bed. Owen Owen's large store in the city centre had a direct hit.

Wednesday 9 October:　　They were at Birmingham again, the guns going all night. I felt nervous in the house, so slept in the shelter.

Thurday 10 October:　　Another quiet night, but poor Birmingham. I hope Joyce is safe.

Friday 11 October:　　Still Birmingham.

Saturday 12 October:　　Still Birmingham.

Sunday 13 October:　　We had it again last night — same time, 8 pm till about 3 am. The guns were terrific. A new one in the field off Allesley Old Road near to us makes more noise than a bomb. I am as much afraid of shrapnel as of incendiaries. Red hot pieces of metal can slice through the roofs or flesh. They rattle on the tiles all night.

Monday 14 October:　　We called round to see Ted's mother. She was terribly upset. She was in the house alone last week, on the Saturday. She and Brenda are coming round tonight to go into the shelter with me. Sirens went again about 8 pm. I was glad they were with me, as bombs dropped on the Maudsley Road Garage, also Worthingtons opposite the Co-op and the top of Oldfield Road, near to me.

Tuesday 15 October:　　There is only room in the shelter for Mrs Johnson, Barry and her niece Ivy since Ted's mother and Brenda came. Another bad night. The All Clear went about 3 am. Mother and Brenda then slept in my back bed.

Wednesday 16 October:　　The sirens go about ten minutes earlier each night and stay on later into the mornings. 4.30 am when we went to bed. Dora has been sharing a shelter with some neighbours, but is very nervous and is going to Matlock as soon as possible. There is a great deal of damage all over Coventry.

Thursday 17 October:　　Still another air raid. Mrs Johnson stays in the house to keep Ken company. She wants to get a house in the country. I have written to Sheila about one for her. I shall stay and see it through. Besides, it is my duty to stay to see to Ted.

From now onwards we have the sirens every night, sometimes it is Birmingham or West Bromwich, sometimes Coventry. The nearest bomb to us was in Dulverton Avenue and the bottom of Oldfield Road, near the bridle path. Dora has gone to Matlock. The Johnsons go to sleep at a house at Balsall Common. Mrs Probert came to ask me if she and Molly could come into my shelter. Theirs has filled with water and Charles is on duty at the warden's post at the Three Spires Hotel. It is now 31 October 1940.

Saturday 1 November: Mrs Probert has taken Molly to Cheltenham to her husband's mother. That leaves Mother, Brenda and me in the shelter.[22]

From the *Midland Daily Telegraph* war diary

23 October [1940]:   Start of the local 'blitzkrieg'.

24 October: So heavy were the raids becoming that there was something like a mercy evacuation by all people whose work or other duties did not keep them in the city. Every outgoing train and bus was packed. Special buses were run by private operators to the country districts immediately outside the city every night until the All Clear. The roads were filled with private cars as it was getting dusk, all being driven to the safer areas for the night. Many people, rather than stay in the city, slept in the open. On this night (which is probably the 24th) the railway company could not cope with the number of people and hundreds were turned back to the shelters in Greyfriars Green.[93]

Fear and destruction escalate

Les and I were among the audience at the Gaumont Cinema one evening in October when the Alert sounded and the manager interrupted the programme to announce that bombers were overhead in some force, and he considered it to be safer if the audience remained inside the cinema. We thought otherwise and, tin hats in place, were leaving by the main doors when bombs came whistling down. Les, who was just ahead, threw himself flat as I dived for the floor behind him. High explosives blasted property about two hundred yards away and, with mounting experience, we reckoned that distance to be in the "miss as good as a mile" category. We set off for home.

In Gosford Street we overtook a woman groping in the blackness and rather fearful of what she might find when she turned into the communal courtyard shared with the homes of her neighbours. We picked our way with her, over chunks of debris, and noticed the smell of leaking gas. However, she found *her* house to be intact. We returned to our road to Stoke, wondering why the raiders were following *us!*

We ducked again after turning from Far Gosford Street into Binley Road, and sheltered under the garden hedge behind the wall of one of the dentists' houses by Gulson Road. The noisy, shell-lit sky, bright now with the criss-cross beams of probing searchlights, was too alarming for further progress. We slipped with relief into the public air raid shelters dug into the recreation ground at the junction with Humber Road. No cinematic drama could equal the live show going on outside that night for heart-stopping thrills and sustained suspense.

From that night on, except for nights when Les was on duty, we gravitated to that point of the road and its shelter, as if drawn by a magnet. Because it survived evermore frequent air raids on the town, we endowed it with an invisible shield of safety. Our group met there nightly, at the same time and at the same place in the long tunnels. That section became our private domain.

By the end of October, we did not wait for the sirens to sound their warning, but made tracks as soon as we had finished our evening meal, after the day's work was done. Chess might be played by Ron Smith, if he found a partner; usually we played a hand of cards, read the evening paper, exchanged gossip, larked about, and left the shelter briefly to extinguish incendiary bombs which burned harmlessly, having fallen onto the bowling green on the other side of the road.

But one night even our section shook when a bomb hit the far end, causing casualties and one death. The blast had been easily absorbed by the well-designed structure, and a rescue team which trooped past declined our offer of help……

When I cycled to the *Telegraph* each morning, new gaps in the streets, crumbled shops and houses, were seen or heard about. How quickly we adjusted to being bombed regularly. We knew that the factories, all switched to aircraft or other war production, made the town a top target. Similar centres throughout the country now shared this way of life: work, rest when possible, shake off fatigue, eat, work on. When morning bulletins broadcast over the radio that London, West Midlands towns, South Coast ports, Clydeside or Merseyside areas had been bombed, we were braced by the bond that had been forged in the face of common danger.[98]

Lullaby of Indifference?

Two reports from early in November confirm the toll the German bombers had already taken on Coventry and the extent of the escalation and intensity of the Autumn raids:

Private and confidential

The Council House
Coventry
12 November 1940

Dear Mr Taylor,

Thank you for your letter of 11 November concerning the proposal of your committee to analyse the effects of the air raids on Coventry. So far as the casualties are concerned the figures up to date are:

Killed	180
Injured and treated in hospital	265
Injured and treated at first aid posts	485

These figures are confidential and should not be published or divulged. The population of Coventry so far as one can tell is in the region of 250,000.

Yours faithfully,

Arthur Massey
Medical Officer of Health
and Director of Emergency
Medical Services

J Taylor, Esq,
Honorary Secretary,
Coventry Information Committee,
10a Hay Lane,
Coventry.[90]

Ministry of Information
Facts concerning the city

Population	260,000 (estimate)
Area of city	19,167 acres
Number of factories	300 (approx)
Number of insured population	120,000
Number of houses	70,000
Number of warnings in the city	250 (approx)
Number of actual raids on the city	25
Number of factories hit	12 (approx)
Number of persons killed	180
Number of persons injured and treated in hospital	265
Number of persons injured and treated at first aid posts	485
Number of first aid posts	5
Houses either demolished or so badly damaged as to be uninhabitable	350 to 400
Houses damaged, but repairable	6,000[95]

With the build up in air raids, what was the response of the local Civil Defence and the Emergency Committee?

The Air Raid Precaution services were organised into five sections. The Engineering Service consisted of gas decontamination parties, rescue parties and demolition parties, under the City Engineer. The Emergency Medical Service consisted of the two base hospitals, the Coventry and Warwickshire and the Gulson, with their emergency staff, first aid posts and mobile first aid parties organised to deal with casualties in every area of the city.

The third service was the Emergency Fire Service, which included both the regular fire brigade and the Auxiliary Fire Service, and had fire patrol units and fire posts across the city.

The most important service was the Air Raid Warden system controlled by the Chief Constable. Each warden's post was equipped with a telephone and was required to assess each emergency and to call in the relevant specialised emergency units. The fifth arm was the Emergency Transport and Communication Service, with responsibility to provide effective transport and communication facilities to each of the other services. There was also a well organised control system co-ordinating them all.

The city was divided into six areas:
1. Central
2. Foleshill and Bell Green
3. Radford and Allesley
4. Earlsdon and Westwood
5. Cheylesmore and Lower Stoke
6. Upper Stoke and Wyken

Every area was under the supervision of a Zone Controller, assisted by Zone Directors from each service, all in direct contact with their Chief Director. In all, they organised 6,698 volunteers, 2,646 of whom were in the Air Raid Warden service.

From 1939, these services came under the control of the Coventry Emergency Committee, which was kept in daily touch by the ARP Controller. At the outbreak of war, precautions were immediately started. The factories were circularised and ordered to provide adequate shelters, bomb and fire protection for their workers. Anderson shelters were issued free. Street shelters were built, although they were to prove pathetically inadequate due to skimping in the use of cement. Complexes of underground shelters, some of which could hold up to twelve thousand people, were constructed. By the week before the November blitz, places had been provided for 80,920 in Anderson shelters, 24,230 in communal domestic surface shelters, and 34,791 could be accommodated in underground public shelters.

As well as building shelters, people at particular risk were evacuated. Priority was given to children, infants and their mothers, pregnant women and some invalids, including the blind. The central area of Coventry was defined as an evacuation area and 8,000 applied to be evacuated, mainly to the north and south of Warwickshire, although many were slow to be found places and some of those who were, drifted back in the relative calm of the Summer of 1940.

There were twelve or thirteen [accounts vary] rest centres provided, mostly in church halls, equipped with blankets, clothing and hot food. They were designed to shelter the homeless temporarily after raids. However, the standard of the centres was not always up to people's expectations.

In addition, there was a range of grants, aid agencies and government services to help people in need. Homeless people could apply for clothing vouchers to get emergency clothes from the Women's Voluntary Service at Drapers Hall, given by the Mayor's Fund for Relief of Air Raid Distress, set up in October 1940. Funeral expenses would also be paid in exceptional circumstances, such as death from pneumonia through exposure after a raid. There were emergency feeding centres, one of which was at the Technical College on The Butts, with free vouchers given out by the rest centres. There was a Messenger Motorbike Service, a Food Contamination Service and specific assembly points for those made homeless.

There was an extensive system of Air Raid Wardens' posts in schools, hotels, libraries, churches and 'structures'. Also provided were emergency hostels, housing between twenty and forty people, and a government compensation scheme to deal with war damage. People had thirty days to complete a VOW1 claim form.

A billeting officer was appointed by the Emergency Committee to persuade or, if necessary, force people to take in workers from outside the city as boarders. Houses left empty by evacuees were occasionally requisitioned to house them. So preparations were extensive, although, as these excerpts from the minutes of the Coventry Committee of the Ministry of Information show, many pleas to the Government for defence and precautions were not met with in time for the November raid:

National Emergency Committee prepares

26 August [1939]:   a) Coventry is declared a neutral zone under area plan Nº 2. It is later to become an evacuation area.

b) Public shelters in basements are designated. The contract for the construction of trenches is undertaken by Daniels.

29 August: a) The Chief Officer of the fire brigade suggested temporary sluices from the River Sherbourne to provide water for fire fighting......

c) 10% of the population are to be provided for in basement shelters and trenches.

6 September: a) an emergency mortuary for air raid victims was proposed at Priory Street Baths. It was to accommodate five hundred bodies.

18 October: 434 is to be the authorised established Auxiliary Fire Service personnel. At present there are 110.

23 November: a) An emergency mortuary is to be established on Pool Meadow in connection with the one in Priory Street Baths. [A review of ARP personnel, excluding first aid posts and ambulance drivers, showed that, of an Authorised War Establishment requirement of 2,502 part-time and 2,192 full-time personnel, the actual effective establishment was 3,016 part-time and 593 full-time. For the authorised casualty service establishment of 578 part-time and 811 full-time, they had recruited 449 part-timers, but only 356 full-timers.]

25 January [1940]:   b) ......The following proposals have been made: the taking of water from a number of ponds, swimming baths and canals; the provision of temporary dams on the Sherbourne, pending permanent sluice gates; the provision of fire mains and sumps in positions recommended by the Chief Officer of the FB [Fire Brigade]......

21 March: Air raid shelters are to be completed by the end of June. 80% of the population are to be accommodated in public and private shelters.

Accommodation will be provided in Coventry for an estimated number of 196,800 people, 81.3% of the population. In public shelters, work on 28,000 places has been completed, out of a total of 41,000 required. Domestic shelters: 66,659 [places] have been completed and 155,800 are required.

4 April: b) The Priory Street Baths emergency mortuary is to be transfered to a building at Gas Street works[ie the gasworks at Hill Street].

11 April: a) The number of shrouds is increased from 200 to 1,000.

16 May: The Committee did not support the following resolution from the Cumberland County Council: that the Minister of Home Security be informed that the Committee views with concern both the falling off in the number of available ARP personnel and the increasing disinclination of the personnel to attend for lectures and practices, and that it is not possible materially to raise the standard of training unless some obligation is imposed on the part-time personnel to attend lectures and practices.

21 May: An additional emergency mortuary is to be made available in the Corporation's Highway Depot in Leicester Row.

20 August: The great local demand for bricks for houses and shelters is causing difficulty, and it is proposed that the shelter programme be cut. This is not allowed.

12 September: The AFS [Auxiliary Fire Service] is to be increased from 125 people to 250.

10 October: It is proposed that deep shelter and car park accommodation are provided in Greyfriars Green and Gosford Green. Both would accommodate 12,000 people each, and the cost would be £150,000 each.

31 October: There are complaints of conditions in shelters and a sub-committee is set up to inspect them regularly.

5 November: The ARP controller reported on steps taken since the last meeting to obtain military assistance for rescue and demolition parties.

14 November: 170,344 places have been provided in air raid shelters.[97]

Coventry's Emergency Committee received regular reports on public morale and matters of public concern. Extracts from its meeting of 1 November 1940 show this vividly:

1,400 men were at present employed removing debris caused by enemy action, and the matter of military assistance had been brought before Lord Dudley (Regional Commissioner)......

The question of clearing up debris from bombed areas is causing deep dissatisfaction until it is cleared. There remains a doubt about the possibility of bodies being underneath, as many bodies cannot be identified. The Army could be used for this purpose.

The condition of air raid shelters locally is causing alarm.

Too many lights on the main roads from motors and cycles in and around Coventry, which form a splendid target for the enemy......

Outstanding topics of conversation included: air raid dangers and the possibility of protection; the need for urgency in the repair of damaged property; the need for removal of debris and the use of military units for this purpose; raids; shelters not being deep enough; the scarcity of certain foodstuffs; the difficulties of transport and shopping facilities for factory workers; local air raid damage; the apparent lack of a sufficient AA [Anti-Aircraft] barrage; and the movement of Coventry people to the country at night. On the prevailing sentiment about war, the minutes state that:

Many people seem to have expected concentrated bombing to be worse than is actually the case. More people than hitherto now feel that indiscriminate bombing of Berlin would be an unwise policy.

Public are getting rather fed up with the present stage of the war and feel that present happenings are not helping the war effort......

Generally confident of ultimate victory.

Very little actual depression, believing that England will come out on top finally.

The public generally is accepting war conditions as a necessary evil. People are wondering how long the madness is likely to last.

General comments included:

A fortnight ago, when the raid was on and the men were leaving the Humber works at 9 pm, a train standing in the siding at Folly Lane had a window uncovered and a large light showing. The men were disgusted and wondered if this was allowed.

There is a marked increase in anxiety noticable here:

A large number of people are leaving Coventry each night in cars, trains and on foot, to spend the night in the country, on account of the bombing. These people leave the responsibility of their houses with neighbours or ARP wardens. The danger of fire in unattended premises is great and, as the Government has ordered that business premises should not be left unattended, there is a feeling of resentment among the remaining population that the same order does not apply to private houses, and that some people should so shirk their responsibility as members of a community.

Sentiments are coloured by the prevailing circumstances. We have an air raid here, hours of bombing, damage to houses, many casualties, nerves strained to breaking point, playing havoc with public morale; no apparent effective opposition. Flying round for half an hour and an hour without any anti-aircraft fire. Filthy shelter accommodation. No trench wardens' service. Air raid wardens service totally inadequate. Whole areas being evacuated because of delayed action bombs; housed in bleak church halls; no sleeping accommodation; no real cooking facilities for numbers of people. These things can be put right by a review of the ARP services. Not by the officials, as they know nothing about the jobs, but meet the warden, the first aid man, the rescue man, to discuss ARP.

An organised evacuation of the women and children outside the town is absolutely essential. Men in the ARP services who are on duty in air raids night after night, in AFS Rescue and First Aid Parties, warden service, etc, should not have to worry about their families, whom they have had to leave at home.

Certain cafés in the city must be detailed to stand by on the Red Warning, ready to supply any area with hot meals.

Greece — is she an asset or a liability?

Should works carry on at night till danger signal?

The closing of Centaur Road Station for so long, leaving that side of the city badly provided for in the case of sudden emergency.[95]

A week later, the minutes expressed further concerns, often foretelling the problems the emergency services actually had on the night of the blitz:

The thousands of idle soldiers in the country should be put to work, clearing debris, helping the Civil Defence personnel, etc.

Where has the machinegun defence gone from Coventry? Why not have an English fighter squadron for our defence?

An active local grievance — the protection given to Coventry from enemy air attacks and siren warnings.

Outstanding topics of conversation this week included: that a night fighter squadron patrol the district; where to go to take shelter at night; that car lights should be extinguished on ascending hills; that more petrol should be given to war workers and less to the élite; enemy air attacks; siren warnings; the bombing of Italy; and is Greece a turning point in the war?

Prevailing sentiment and concerns about the war centred on:

Entrance of Greece into the war would appear to make action against Italy more effective.

Since the invasion of Greece, people seem more optimistic of our ultimate and not so far distant victory.

It has proved to be very outstanding that war workers cannot obtain enough spirit to run their cars to and from work and keep good time, whereas a businessman can obtain spirit and use same for pleasure trips and running away from night raiders. Bevin says, "You must not let my army down". Yet one hears that the local Transport Committee is turning down volunteer drivers to get the workers to "Go to it".

The public are desirous of knowing how it is that enemy aeroplanes can come over in broad daylight and drop bombs and machinegun the public from a low altitude, without even a siren warning that they are in the vicinity.[95]

Finally, the minutes of the meeting held on the day of the raid itself, Thursday 14 November 1940, list local grievances and make, at times, sad reading:

Wet condition of shelters, and animals and children making a convenience of same.

The scarcity of certain commodities is causing a great deal of discussion amongst housewives. It is felt that, in certain circumstances, the rationing system should be extended to create a wider distribution. Goods such as jams, biscuits, tinned milk, cheese, currants, raisins, canned peas, and candles are mentioned as very difficult to purchase.

The Government's shelter policy should be overhauled or plans made for the nightly evacuation of workers. The shelters at present are death traps and more people may die of pneumonia through going into wet shelters than have ever been killed by bombs.

Local grievance about air raid shelters and the nightly evacuation of able-bodied men and women from the city. A grievance also about the Government's reluctance to state its war aims.

Very concerned about daylight raiders.

Why aren't hours staggered, so that people can catch buses?

Lack of anti-aircraft protection and the fact that lone raiders can hover overhead in daylight for three quarters of an hour without attack, with the result that thousands, including production workers, are leaving the city.

Discontent of the work people and threats being used of a strike, if no effort is made to ensure their safety from machinegun fire.

Outstanding topics of conversation still included air raids; repairs to property; the state of the shelters; and the need to improve the anti-aircraft barrage. The list goes on:

Condemnation of exodus from Coventry at night.
What is it all for and what is to be the outcome of the present misery and suffering?
The inadequacy of the Services to deal with after-effects of air raids quickly, especially against weather on personal belongings.

Improvement in the anti-aircraft barrage.
The need of measures to deal with enemy single raiders in daylight.
Insufficient defence against bombing......
Transport problems.
More amenities for Civil Defence workers, and increased personnel for same.

Prevailing sentiment and general comments about the War were a mixture of weariness and hope that the worst was over:

Very optimistic since Greek successes. [The Greeks had reversed the Italian advance from Albania.] Not expected to be over soon, but have yet to meet the person who considers we shall go under.

The majority still feel they must grin and bear it. People seem to realise the necessity now more than ever of seeing it through.

Optimism with regard to war in Greece and a feeling that the worst of the "blitz" is over [!]

There is a feeling of discontent at the present stage of the war, intensified no doubt by the winter weather, which causes added suffering to the poorest classes, already the chief victims......

There is a recovery of morale immediately following a night free from raids and an improvement in barrage against aircraft......

There is a good deal of dissatisfaction about the state of the factories in the city. Men are having days off because of shortage of materials. Are we short of materials or not? The public morale is fairly good, but it will not remain so if work gets short and wages consequently fall. The public can stand a certain amount of inconvenience if their wages allow them a few extra comforts and luxuries. Wealthy people are able to leave raided areas, or have comfortable shelters built, but, as usual in war, the poorer classes are the greatest sufferers......

The Government, it is felt, should extend its power in the price fixing of articles. Most commodities today are in short supply and in many instances are sold to the highest bidder. Distribution has become somewhat disorganised owing to evacuation on a very much larger scale.[95]

As is evident from the above reports, many precautions were well under way, but there was still inadequate defence in many areas. The main areas of concern which specifically related to air raid precautions were the lack of ARP personnel, the state of the shelters and the lack of air defence. There were few anti-aircraft guns and, according to reports, they were to run out of shells at some time after midnight during the great blitz. There was also a startling lack of RAF fighters to combat the enemy.

Whilst the Luftwaffe rapidly built up the number of raids on the city,

Coventry's Emergency Committee struggled to meet targets for precautions and tried its best to cope with people's criticisms and warnings, in turn passing on its own misgivings to the Government.

That the inadequacy of the air defences was a frequently stated worry of many people in the city is evident from the reports on public morale, no doubt being a major cause for the nightly exodus, with people "voting with their feet", as it were. Sometimes the sirens failed to go off. Lone daytime raiders were left to strafe and bomb at will and without opposition; anti-aircraft guns sometimes failed to even open up against the enemy. But how much of the sense of bitterness and accusation after 14 November arose from frustration at the scale of the horrific onslaught, which defeated all efforts to save the situation?

Doubtless, these were frustrations which affected more places than Coventry, made worse by the tremendous strain the Battle of Britain and London Blitz had put on British fighters in the Summer and Autumn. It should not be forgotten that most of the local squads and services set up in the city seemed confident of being well organised and prepared.

The Decontamination Squads, Gas Identification Service and Food Contamination Service, though fortunately not yet called upon to function, are nevertheless organised for immediate and efficient action.

They are thoroughly well trained and equipped, and although it is fervently hoped that none of these services will ever be needed, the deep conviction is that the utmost reliance could be placed upon these services.[117]

Furthermore, the reports (see final chapter) from the Chief Fire Officer, the Water Department, the Gas Company and the Civil Defence all suggest the city was, generally speaking, as well prepared as was possible, or even as was necessary. The emergency services were dealing with remorseless pressure as well as they could:

The frequent and continuous hours of duty imposed a terrific strain on all members of these services, and particularly was this so during the October 1940 raids, when for many consecutive nights they were on duty incessantly without rest. These facts should be borne in mind when considering the wonderful work of all the Civil Defence members during and after the raid of 14 November. They all rose nobly to the tremendous demands made upon them and no praise is too high for the results they achieved.[117]

The smouldering ruins of Broadgate

Death March

(Air raid log — 14 November 1940)

20.30   N° 6 reports small red flashes from behind St Paul's tower, Foleshill, about 100 — 200 feet; light soon goes. Also seen by N° 1 Post (Entwistle) in centre of town while explosive incendiaries were around, coming from all directions.

            (Entwistle) N° 1 Post sees land mine coming down by parachute.

20.56   Phone out of order and tower vacated!

20.59   (Entwistle) N° 1 Post revisits tower and reports huge fires, many HEs, land mines, etc, and vacates tower.

21.00   Tower hit by HE?

21.30   Building shook many times and fires are being allowed to burn and develop as fire brigades have insufficient water pressure, owing to mains being hit.

00.12   Light failed! The city is now without electricity, gas, water, and many roads are blocked.

00.15   Fires developing all over city centre and uncontrolled!

00.16   Part of Cathedral roof falls in.[23]

Unforgettable horror

By now the raid was growing in intensity — the full fury of the attack reaching its height with a savagery of bombing of almost unbelievable ferocity. A night of unforgettable horror — the scream of falling bombs — the shattering explosions — the showers of incendiaries, literally thousands, and then the, perhaps, most horrifying sight of all — the sudden fires leaping up, their flames, fanned by the wind, rapidly spreading and enveloping all within reach. The agony of helplessly watching valuable buildings being consumed by the raging fires, and being powerless to prevent their destruction, was almost beyond the limit of human endurance.[88]

It was a night of horror that none would ever forget. Gunner William Davies, on ten days' leave, stumbled over a prostrate body in Hertford Street and recoiled aghast — then realised it was one of the city's three statues of Peeping

Tom. Along with a colleague, Daimler's Labour Manager, Leslie Wale, he tussled for minutes on end to free a signalman on the railway embankment near by. Telephone wires had fallen to enmesh the man from head to foot like an escapologist. Ambulance driver Wilfred Bevan recovered one torso so maimed that only the absence of genitals told him that this had been a woman; bomb blast had concertinaed both stomach and breasts. At Courtauld's, Fire Officer Bert Bucknall and his mate Cecil Heward were buried by blast astride the main steam duct to the nylon factory, the scalding steam playing like a geyser's jet on Bucknall's legs and Heward's head.

Both men were to survive — though Bucknall was to endure twenty-six plastic surgery operations and Heward, for whom surgeons fashioned a new face, a new ear and new thumbs, double that number.

Everywhere, there were alien sights......drifting barrage balloons bobbing like giant whales at roof top level......a kitten patting absorbedly at charred scraps of paper floating across the gardens......a length of streetcar track sailing twenty clear yards like a monstrous rocket, clean over a three storey house. Landlord Harry Ward emerged from his pub cellar, where he had taken shelter, then ran for his life; a knee-high river of boiling butter from a dairy near by was coursing down the street.

At [-] Beechwood Avenue, William Heynes, a Liaison Officer with Short's Aircraft, was fascinated by what seemed like a large tree felled across the road — a trunk almost twelve feet long, two feet in diameter.

"Come and see this," he called to Dorothy, his wife. Then, a second later, "Get back — there's a mine outside!"

At that moment, a thunderclap of sound, 1,560 lbs of high explosive went sky-high, bursting Heynes' eardrum, burying him upside down in blue clay, showering Dorothy with broken glass, and killing outright their four-year-old son, Simon, who was crouched beneath the stairs.[21]

Caught above ground level in a tree or on some building, these diabolical weapons did not waste any of their energy like bombs, digging holes in the ground. The blast from them travelled laterally and could fell whole rows of houses.

I stepped out into the garden and there, over to the east, was something looking like an iron bedstead. It was floating down on four parachutes and there were lights on the thing......

That particular mine, clearly visible because the night was a bright one, dropped in nearby fields. Although almost rooted to the spot by the spectacle, I did not wait to see what happened next. I did the only thing possible, went to ground quickly, hurrying into the shelter with my new baby.[51]

In a very short time the glow of the sky told us that major fires had been started, the sound of plane engines was incessant and the bombs rained down on us. The noise was terrific. One dropped very close and the blast blew us over, despite our being inside the Anderson shelter.

We later found that five houses across the way had been flattened, killing two of our neighbours. There was no let up in the bombing, wave after wave of planes going over. We could even hear the bomb doors opening and then that terrible whistle as the bombs hurtled down on their journey of death and destruction.

It was said that one never heard the whistle of the bomb that killed one; I think that fable was put about by the Ministry of Information to boost morale!

During this raid, the fire watchers thought that we were being invaded, as a parachute was spotted floating above the end of our street. The Home Guard fired at it but, luckily for us, they were rotten aimers. As the 'chute got lower, we could see that a large coffin-shaped object was attached to it and it was thought to be carrying supplies for the invaders.

It landed across the main road and they dragged it to one side so that the way would be clear for the ambulances. A warden arrived on the scene, recognised the object as a land mine and ordered the immediate evacuation of the area. We were told to leave the street at the end farthest away from the mine, and hurry.

Just as a large number of us had reached the bottom of the street, a high explosive came whistling down, obviously heading our way. We threw ourselves to the ground. There was a rushing noise, followed by a deafening explosion, but miraculously no one was hurt. The gas main at the street corner was on fire and flames were shooting in the air as high as the houses.

"Run for your lives!" shouted the wardens. "Find shelter anywhere away from here!"

In the confusion, families got separated and two neighbours' children were standing bewildered and frightened. Dad and I could not see their parents, so we grabbed them by the hand and ran. We eventually got to a public shelter about a mile away, where there was room to cram more in.

Piles of rubble and glass were everywhere. All the telephone wires were down and fires raged all about the area. It was during this flight that I received my war wound! I tripped over and some wire stuck into my leg, leaving a small scar, which I still have.

When we reached the shelter, there was a small crater in the road outside the entrance to the shelter. A few days later I heard that it had been caused by a delayed action bomb which was later dismantled by the Army Bomb Disposal Unit.

People were pouring into the shelter as different areas were being evacuated. We were all packed like sardines.[58]

We could see the planes clearly. We stood outside the shelter calling them everything and they must have seen us as, when they came down low, we could see them in the cockpit.

We didn't bother to go into the shelter again, as all fear had left us and we did not care any more. Lots of people that night got past bothering about themselves. They just did everything for the dying and injured.

I'll never forget, while we were standing outside the shelter we saw something that looked like a German with a parachute falling from the sky. We picked up sticks, as it looked as if it was coming our way. Then the wind changed.

Minutes after that, there was a terrific explosion. It was a land mine and it had landed farther up the street. The men ran out into the street, wondering what it was, touched it, and were blown to bits. The young boy who sat next to me in school had his father killed in that terrible tragedy, and a lot more got killed that I knew. They were terrible things, those mines.[64]

All hell let loose

I made my way to Clarendon Street, Earlsdon, to my future wife's home, as she was holding a belated birthday gathering with a few friends.

Half an hour after I arrived, the first drone started and then all hell was let loose. All dived under the table; with the drinks, I might add! Suddenly, there was a terrific explosion; one of the houses nearby was hit and the back window was blown in where I was. I said I was going out to see what I could do, much against my friends' advice.

The whole of the centre of the city was in flames and the air was filled with smoke and acrid fumes. I was half way up the street when an old couple came up to me and the lady said, could I help her husband to get to hospital. I said I couldn't, as all the streets were blown up and nothing could get through the flames. Then I looked up and there, protruding from his eye, was a six inch dart of glass!

Nearing the top of the street, an old lady came sobbing to me and asked if I would help her husband. "Of course, "I said. "Where is he?"

"Under the door," she said. "Number Fifty-one."

Funny now, not funny then!

Slowly, I made my way to the top of Earlsdon Street, to the tram terminus. There was a great hole in the road, with a double decker bus in it!

I moved along to where a house had only a few minutes earlier been demolished by a direct hit. I know I was in a state of shock, but was still sure of myself. I imagined things, but not this. There was a cry from under the rubble, so, with my bare hands, I dug a young woman out.

"My baby," she said. "My baby, get my baby!"

"Where is it?" I asked.

"Under the stairs," she said.

Luckily, the stairs were left; unluckily, the baby was dead, the blast bursting its lungs, I found out later. I wandered around and came to Spencer Park and saw a body covered with a tarpaulin. Pulling back the covering from the face, I was grieved to see one of my best friends from our unit. As in a dream, I staggered back to my unit......

When one has seen little children trying to break a way through a brick wall with their hands, as I did on the night of the 'civilian' raid, then maybe you'll understand......[7]

Cellar sanctuaries

Jessie Shuttleworth, recently married and just moved to Lower Ford Street, had rushed into the shelter of her cellar at 7 o'clock:

Now, down the cellar. I took my two cats and all I'd got for light were three candles. The Corporation had been in previously and knocked out the walls so that I could bash the bricks in the wall and get through, in an attempt to escape.

Anyway, I was down there all night long. Ten hours actually. And my neighbours, the Browns, kept tapping the wall and saying, "Are you all right?", "Shall I knock the wall through?"

I said, "No, no."

So then Mr Brown said, "Look, come round here and we'll see if we can get a cup of tea for you."

So I came up the cellar stairs to find that the door was hanging off and the windows were blown in. The boiler house from BTH [British Thompson Houston] had had a direct hit, shattering us with all these metal parts. As I proceded through the door to come round to his gate he met me, but the sight I will never forget as long as I live. There was water running down the streets, fire, what looked like tracer bullets across the sky. It was a fantastic sight, and yet it was so eerie.[111]

My mother and father kept the Three Shuttles Inn in Howard Street at the time and every night during the blitz the small cellar of the pub was crowded with people sheltering from the raids. We played bingo, or housey-housey as it was called then, to pass away the time. On the night of 14 November 1940 we were in the cellar from 7 pm to 7 am the next morning. The electricity all went off and we had candles stuck on top of the beer barrels as our only means of light. How we survived that night was a miracle, as it seemed almost every home around us was destroyed. When we emerged from the cellar, the scene was one of utter devastation.[75]

I spent the early evening and night of this blitz starting out in the crypt of the Old Cathedral, until we were evacuated to the cellar of the Drapers Hall, the door of the entrance to which can still be seen from St Mary's Street.[20]

Fleeing through Broadgate

Broadgate received the brunt of the early bombing as it was pulverised by incendiaries and high explosives. There were few major factories here, apart from Triumph's, where the De Vere Hotel and swimming baths now stand. So it was obviously designed to wipe the city centre off the map. Those trapped around Broadgate had the worst time of all:

The only refuge we had was the cellar, but eventually we had to leave it. The heat from the city, burning all about us, made it too hot to stay. For some time we couldn't get out, because the entrance was blocked by burning timber and fallen stone and bricks. It wasn't until 1.30 am that, by a superhuman effort, I heaved up the iron drop gates which led from the cellar into the hotel yard.

We tried to escape from the crashing, burning building by running through the yard and along the passage which led to Broadgate. We were met by a river of burning butter and fat flowing from the Maypole [Dairy].

It was terrifying! We rushed to escape by the only way now open to us, through the burning hotel itself. The building was now just a heap of blazing ruins, but we made it to the Market Square. The roar of the flames, the crash of bombs, the scorching heat, made our position seem hopeless. Yet we still aimed at getting through to Broadgate and the crash of a bursting petrol tank in a burning bus in Market Square lent speed to our feet.

I shall never forget that awful dash for shelter, leading my wife through masses of red-hot debris and fallen tramway wires. She had a tin basin on her head and I had an enamel bucket on mine. I'm sure that, if we hadn't had these for protection, we'd have been left without a hair on our heads.

Once in Broadgate, we worried about our daughter. The people occupying the shelter to which she had gone had all been moved to a safer place. We couldn't find her and so we made our way to the fire station. Nearby, we found a shelter where we could rest until daybreak.[28]

I was walking through Broadgate on my way home...... past the old Lyons Café, when the warden said to me, "Where' you going, miss?"

So I said, "I'm going home."

So he said, "No you're not, you're coming in here," because the sirens had already gone at a couple of minutes [past] seven.

So I went inside. There were a lot more people in there. Young children, babies. I sat down on the concrete seats that were there and stayed there until practically half way through the night.

It was getting worse, and there was an RAF man, only a young lad, a dark, curly haired chap. He'd got an accordion and was playing to keep us all from being afraid. He was great......

We heard this terrific crash and, evidently, all Lyons Café was on fire, the ceiling had started to come down and all the cement was flying everywhere. We couldn't breathe. One of the wardens came in and wet our lips...... because we had no water. It was terrible, the bangs; everyone was screaming and then they told us we'd got to evacuate. So they told us we all had to help to make this hole in the wall. We kicked it and thumped it and knocked it.

Anyhow, eventually we made a big hole, big enough for us to go through. Ten of us had to form a human chain; a child, an old person, a young person, so we could help each other. He told us we'd got to run round the back of the Cathedral to the air raid shelter opposite Much Park Street.

We formed the chain in tens and when we got outside it was terrible. The sky was lit up, there were incendiary bombs falling everywhere, there were hot cinders and bangs and flashes and everything was on fire. We ran all the way through it. Our little party got there safely and we went down into this shelter. There was a warden standing outside, on the bottom step. He fetched us in and they gave us hot cocoa and blankets to put round us.

I had a couple of burns — one on each foot from hot cinders and a burn on my forehead, but nothing really serious. Otherwise, we were all right and we stayed there until the All Clear went.[19]

At two o'clock in the morning, a policeman on duty came and told us the shop above us was on fire and we had all got to get out, but only two at a time. We were directed to Anslow's shelter in the High Street, and I am pleased to say we all got there safely. While we were down there, the blast from a bomb blew the door off and it hit my elbow.

After the All Clear, we were shocked at the state of everything all around us, and the one thing on my mind was my family, who lived at [-] The Bull Yard.

I hurried home, down Hertford Street, and saw the house was intact. When I got to the gate, I was stopped by a neighbour, to be told my Mum, Dad, and two sisters had been killed, as the shelter they went in had received a direct hit and there were no survivors.[118]

Incendiaries poured down upon us before the Alert had sounded and, as the age of chivalry had not yet passed, my prime object was to make sure that I got her [his cinema usherette date] safely to her home in the Humber Road area.

Little did I realise that the mile or so nightmare journey was going to take us ten hellish-long hours stumbling and tumbling among the debris from one shelter to another en route, and giving help to anyone in need. Bombs exploded around us; buildings burned fiercely; houses tumbled and gas and water pipes burst and exploded, causing mud and stench everywhere......

A solitary figure in factory overalls emerged like a ghost out of the swirling, smelly smoke before me. He was swearing and grumbling that "this bloody lot" was going to make him late for work. I had to smile, but this was the true spirit of war-time Coventry......

I remember looking with horror into the huge bomb crater, the edge of it only a few feet away from the shelter in which my parents and neighbours had spent the night. It was a miracle that the blast had missed them and that they were all safe.[45]

I then thought of going home to see how the family were coping. On passing the new, partly-built Herbert Art Gallery, a land mine went off between the art gallery and Council House, blowing me off my feet and tearing my suit. I think I was more concerned about this and the reception I would get at home than I was with the bombs coming down.

I still remember doing a little more wandering around Much Park Street. All the houses in a large courtyard, which I believe were all solicitors' and doctors' houses, had a large number of stirrup pumps and buckets lying around abandoned.

My family were not at home, but I found my mother and father in the foyer of the Gaumont. A bomb had just dropped on the stage of the Gaumont and I found out that my brother had been injured and the friend he was talking to had been killed. It was four days before we found my brother. He had been taken by ambulance to Dudley......

I also remember being asked to help further up Jordan Well, just past the Dun Cow, as a bomb had fallen on a shelter. Several people were killed.

The fires on both sides of Jordan Well were put out, but due to lack of water the flames started up again and several more shops and houses were burnt down on the fifteenth. One of these, I remember, was the Maddox and Spade public house.[54]

In the very heart of medieval Coventry, breathing the spirit of the past, was the ancient Palace Yard, a quaint quadrangle of half-timbered buildings of the Elizabethan age, once the home of the Hopkins family, to whose memory a marble monument appeared in the Cathedral.

Of very great historical interest, the mansion gave hospitality to many royal personages. It is reputed that the Princess Elizabeth, daughter of James I, was entertained here for a night in 1605, being removed from Coombe Abbey on the discovery of the Gunpowder Plot. James II held his Court here in 1687 and the Princess Anne, later Queen, was lavishly entertained in 1688. A visit from Prince George of Denmark followed in 1690.

Apart form some splendid leadwork, including the Hopkins arms on a lead spout on the east side, the exterior suffered sadly from neglect. The interior, however, testified to the former grandeur and beauty of the building, in the once magnificent banqueting hall, an apartment with a beautiful panelled plaster ceiling and a fine fifteenth century stone chimney piece.

This, typical of many such "military objectives" attacked by the Germans, was utterly and completely destroyed in the heavy raid of 14 November 1940, only a shapeless heap of debris remaining to mark the spot where once stood the proud relic of a bygone age.[108]

Cathedral death throes

"We've been doing our best to get hold of a fire brigade, but they're all out fighting the fires already," a police officer brought word to them. "The Solihull fire brigade is trying to get here, but there are great holes in the roads that no vehicle can get by, and many of the streets are blocked with fallen buildings."

At last, at 9.30 pm, the Solihull fire brigade did arrive and the Cathedral guard took fresh heart. The brigade had come by a round about route, having had narrow escapes from falling walls on the way. Quickly, they fitted up their lengths of hose and the four fire watchers, weary though they were, lent a helping hand. Jock Forbes, who knew every inch of the building, was able to guide them up and down the ladders and roofs......

Soon a jet of water was playing on the fire, which was raging over a large part of the roof. Some of the flaming wood had fallen through into the pews below and set them alight. All the same, the steady jets of water were beginning to slow down the rapid spread of the flames a little, when the fireman who was holding the end of the hose gave a cry of dismay.

"Where's the water gone?" he exclaimed.

The jet had changed from a strong flow to a tiny stream and thence to a mere trickle. Then it stopped altogether......

Soon, the fire was raging once more, the Provost and other guards trying to save what valuable church items they could, the firemen trying to repair the burst main. The water came on for a few minutes around 10.30 pm, but by then the Cathedral was doomed.

By midnight, every roof had fallen in, every pillar had collapsed, every scrap of woodwork had been burnt to ash. The Cathedral lay open to the sky with its burning, smouldering debris lying within the shell of its outer walls. Only the tower and spire stood erect. [49]

Foleshill shelter blasted

The bottom of the Foleshill Road, around Courtaulds, Cash's and the streets from the canal down to Eagle Street and Bishopsgate Green was another area which received intense bombardment, perhaps second only to the city centre. Several witnesses, including ambulance drivers, describe this area, unfortunately close to the Coventry and Warwickshire Hospital, as an inferno.

The area had a shelter built in an old, three storey warehouse opposite George Eliot Road, off the Foleshill Road, which was built to accommodate three hundred. This night it was crammed with five hundred who had fled the bombs and their besieged homes.

It was worse than hell in our shelter, which was now like a cage of frightened [animals]...... people did as the wardens told them and were led to the far end of the shelter, away from a time bomb, which at any moment could have destroyed the building. The bomb had smashed downwards through the building like a roaring tornado, shaking the foundations and causing panic among brave people who had stood more than enough already.

At that moment, they didn't know it was a time bomb. Their end could have come at once. When it did finally explode, it killed three people and injured others......It was difficult to make oneself heard above the screaming of the falling bombs, the roar of their explosions and the added din from the anti-aircraft barrage.

The shrill cry of a frightened child was heard quite often. Screaming bombs, fire bombs and time bombs seemed to be dropping all around us. [A gallant nurse cared for the injured and those driven to hysteria by the sight of their crumbling homes.] I remember so well how a young girl sang to keep their spirits up. I admire her to this day......[We heard] that the Daimler was flat to the ground, which upset my mother, knowing two of the family were there. By then the guns had run out of ammunition and there was no chance of bringing up more because the roads were impassable.

Three o'clock in the morning and still we survived while death rained from the skies. One more shattering blow shook the building and later came gallons of water. The canal behind the shelter had been hit and young and old in the shelter were ankle deep. Next, a fire started above the shelter, tackled by volunteers called for by a warden, while those remaining were half-choked by the flames.

And this was while the unexploded time bomb was still keeping everyone in suspense. Most people were so numbed with shock that they remained in the shelter with the time bomb still to go off. I managed to leave my mother to run home and see if our house was still standing, and fortunately it was, but only just. The back of it was ripped away, with the windows, doors and roof non-existent.[128]

I was kept very busy running up and down Ena Road putting out fires. The street was deserted and I got no help all night with fire fighting. It was hopeless, as incendiaries were clattering onto the houses all night, setting fires all around. So I had to try and find help, but all I came across was a lone fireman around the corner on Foleshill Road. I gave him a spell off for about ten minutes, because he wanted to see what was going on. He came back, looking worried, and told me to leave the city because it was going to go on all night. (He was right.)

So I went back to Ena Road and it was now unrecognisable. HE bombs had fallen on it and [-], my digs, was gutted. All this time both HE and fire bombs had been, and were, falling all around the area. I wasn't unduly perturbed, but was in fact annoyed that my new bicycle was smashed in the back yard.

I couldn't get any water now from [-] to fight the fires all around and it was while sitting on the pavement outside, wondering what to do next, that fate took a hand. An unexploded fire bomb rolled towards me, off the road. It was about nine inches long, with a fin. I picked it up out of curiosity, then tossed it away, but it exploded on impact, and my left leg caught the brunt of the shrapnel, which put me out of action. I now had no alternative but to get out of Coventry, if I could, so began a nightmare journey along the Foleshill Road, dragging my injured left leg behind me, with the incessant bombs still exploding all around. It was after midnight, but fortunately an ARP warden spotted me and took me into a nearby clearance station where I stayed until daybreak, when the raiders had, at last, gone.

Inside the clearance station were about two dozen injured persons lying around. The chap next to me was continuously moaning. The harrassed medico told me a wall had collapsed onto him and his legs had had to be amputated when he had been got out.

Bombs had been dropping all around the clearance station, so when I was told that the person on my left was dead, I left the clearance station and was shocked at the scene outside. I dragged myself back to the city centre, but was informed that the General Hospital had been evacuated during the night and to wait, as a shuttle service was in operation, taking casualties to outside hospitals. I finished up in the Coventry and Warwickshire Hospital, and was there nine months.[46]

Versions of hell

Fred Griffin was driving his bus nearby. There were no passengers on board, because everyone who could had gone to earth. But with a bus on their hands, Fred and his conductor, Joe Wright......carried on. Besides, Fred......especially wanted to get home to his wife Hilda, because it was her birthday. He was not to see her until the following day. Meanwhile, each experienced a slightly different version of hell.

While Hilda, covered in dust and soot, crouched beneath the stairs all night with a neighbour in Widdrington Road, Fred watched bombs falling on a city centre dress shop and Owen Owen. A stick of bombs fell along the line of terraced houses in Widdrington Road too and, when Hilda crawled from the refuge the next morning, she found a land mine hanging from the telegraph wires at the back of her house.

Broadgate was a scheduled stop, and Fred stopped. Farther on along his route, he got off the bus near Prince of Wales Road and was blown into a doorway by blast. "We stopped and watched the bombs dropping on the city."

Fred and Joe spent the night with their bus at Allesley.[55]

"Are we downhearted?"

The sounds were the most alarming. The relentless throbbing of the German bombers, particularly on 14 November; the high pitched scream of the bombs, each one seeming to come nearer, not breathing between each, as I clung to my mother, not expecting to live through the night. Hysterical laughter when my sister, who was with neighbours, was rescued from a shelter buried by blast from a bomb nearby. A deathly hush as we climbed into the night air, which was quickly broken by a dull crunch as a pillar of clay rose skywards. It was the first of many delayed actions to explode.

I forget who coined the phrase, "Are we downhearted?", but it came in useful after racing through the flame lit streets to shelter under the BTH factory [British Thompson Houston, in Alma Street], only to be told we were a sitting target. The gun on top was firing. We were hit. When the effects of the blast wore off and the water was rising, through the darkness came the cry, "Are we downhearted?" Although feeble, the answer was, "No!"

The glass crunched under our feet as the gallant ARP chaperoned us to Gosford Green underground shelter, which was a rabbit warren. Only a direct hit, where you stood, could get you. That was good news.

After a trek across the city, tired and numb, we arrived at the comparative safety of Tile Hill. Lying on a relative's floor, we listened to the windows rattle, and to the comforting but frightening sound of the anti-aircraft gun in the woods nearby. There were several of these positioned around the city. They were all nicknamed and the one that comes to mind was "Big Bertha". God bless the men that manned them, for they were fighting a losing battle, but they certainly helped morale.[109]

The Humber like Stonehenge

People from next door came in the small shelter until fourteen in all were in it. Towards twelve o'clock we felt stifled. The Germans dropped bombs unceasingly on the Humber. It seemed as though our last minute had come. The floor shook while the barrage and bombs still fell.

At about two o'clock [some reports say at midnight, others say later than two] the barrage stopped for about an hour [for the rest of the night, according to other accounts] as they had run out of ammunition.

The planes bombed and dive-bombed. Someone happened to open the door of the shelter.

"Good gracious," they cried. "Just look at this."

The sight that met our eyes, if it had been more pleasant, would have been marvellous. The moon was full and high, the sky was a bright red, while the Humber was a blazing inferno......

We heard bricks falling on the shelter and thought it was either our house or [–]'s. Five bangs followed in succession in our road and it seemed like they fell on the shelter. Then a man came to the shelter door and shouted, "Will all the men in this shelter come quickly, as two folks are trapped."

Three men ran out and reassured us that our house was all right, but the road was like a ploughed field. There was a man and a woman trapped four houses down from us, the one next to it having received a direct hit. They could not do anything for the people, as the roof would probably collapse on them, so they had to wait for a rescue squad, all of which were out in the town.

The raid finished at 6.30 am on Friday, the fifteenth. The Humber was like Stonehenge. A bomb hole was outside our house, with destruction all around us. Our house had escaped with guttering down, tiles off and broken windows[121]

Homes destroyed

My father was on nights at the Humber works as a boilerman, therefore my brother and I were responsible for my mother and three smaller children. We had an Anderson shelter in the garden which my father had cemented into the ground, along with our neighbours'.

At seven o'clock the air raid siren sounded. We got my mother, brothers and sister into the shelter, which was about twenty yards from the house. We had nailed benches all round and had a paraffin heater in there.

Plane after plane came droning over, dropping their bombs. It seemed to be all in Coventry centre till about 12 pm, when suddenly a block of incendiaries was dropped on our back garden and next door. My brother and I jumped out with two buckets and placed them on the incendiaries, which blew the buckets up into the air. Being young, it was all a bit of fun to us.

Mr Hayton next door shouted, "Get in the shelter, you silly little devils! The big stuff comes down next!"

We had just got in the shelter when all hell broke loose. Bricks, slates, bottles, masonry, all went flying through the air. It turned out later that a 500 lbs bomb had directly hit our house and took with it two houses on each side, a block of five houses, but the blast had gone directly upwards, not outwards. Not one of us or our neighbours was killed.[82]

On the night of the fourteenth, after several hours above ground, my father went down the shelter we had built in the back garden for a break about 1 am. At 2 am, when climbing up the steps out of the shelter, he was amazed and horrified to see in the bright moonlight, smoke coming out of the lounge chimney pot at the back of the house. Since the fire in the fireplace had been out since 7 pm the previous evening, he immediately concluded that a bomb must have penetrated the house.

He quickly summoned neighbours and they entered to find an incendiary bomb had come through the roof, bedroom ceiling and lounge ceiling and had landed on a pile of cushions. It was one of the explosive type of incendiaries and, had my father entered earlier, he could easily have been injured by the flying shrapnel, as evidenced by the damage to the furniture and walls. Using sandbags and stirrup pumps, they quickly extinguished the fire and undoubtedly saved the house.[107]

Cinemas bombed

Throughout the War, cinemas played a vital part in bolstering morale and helping people forget the tragedy taking place outside. Prior to the blitz, there were huge crowds at the cinemas, with long queues for each showing. During the raids this diminished, but not greatly. They were palaces of escapism. Incredibly, people would continue to sit through the most intense raids, only throwing themselves to the floor at the last moment, as the bombs screamed down. The usherettes couldn't order them out, but could only advise them to leave. This night was no exception, even as the bombs fell.

Florence Barton was working at the Astoria Cinema on Albany Road. As an usherette, she gave the public a choice when there was a raid; using the shelter or staying. A slide went up on the screen with a warning:

You gave them a choice. They could either go to the top of Gosford Green or they could stay in the theatre. Well, we'd got a lovely cellar at the back of the theatre for us staff, but we couldn't go, for the simple reason there was always someone left in, and on the night of the November blitz there were quite a few in, but most of them went up to Gosford Green.

There was a young woman in there with a tiny child in her arms. What the devil she was doing with a child in the cinema, knowing full well that there was bombing going on, I don't know. There was a girl on the other side and there was a man next to me. The one with the baby was killed. The bullet went right through the baby and into the mother, so she was still sitting up there, as upright as anything, with the child in her arms, but she was dead.

On the opposite side in the centre gangway the girl that was sitting there, all her insides were lying on the floor beside her, so that was another one dead......
A man as close as you are to me was killed. I must have been an optimist. I'd

76

got the most awful tummy aches, so I laid flat on the floor. If I'd been sitting up, I wouldn't have had a head, because it went over me and there was a great big hole in the wall...... And the other one was another man. They took him to hospital, but he died during the night, and that was the only five.[16]

And also in a cinema by Spon End:

As usual at that time, when an air raid warning was flashed on the screen, very few people, including yours truly, took any notice of it. However, two hours later, the thirty-odd people who were left had chickened out under the seats of the back row of the cinema and there they stayed for eight very frightening hours.

When I finally emerged at five in the morning, my view through Spon End arches gave me the impression that the whole world was on fire. When I finally found my mother at 7 am in an air raid shelter, she asked me where I had been all night.

"I've been to the pictures, Mum," I replied.[87]

A question of fate

I woke up under loads of debris, being dug out, and was told to keep still until all the bricks had been removed. After some time, I was finally coming out, but could not open my eyes, for all the cuts and dirt in them. Eventually, after all the dirt was away, I looked up to a clear sky. Then my mother, who was an ARP warden at the Stevengraph shelter in Cox Street, was standing there. She borrowed a pushchair and pushed me all the way out to Berkswell to get away.[56]

He was in a team of wardens rushing from place to place, putting out incendiaries. As they raced towards one fire, they had to clamber over rubble from newly collapsed walls in an alleyway.

They were stopped in their tracks when an unseen voice shouted, "Mind where you're treading, I'm under here!"[29]

I believe it's just a matter of fate. I really believe in fate. I think a lot of us did during the war. If a bomb had your name on it, there was nothing you could do about it. I was buried alive and yet I came out of the house. Two friends could just have said goodbye and then a bomb explodes and the blast kills one and hardly touches the other. That's fate. I believe that when your time's up, it's up, and there's nothing you or anyone else can do about it.[47]

Fire fighters vainly trying to douse the flames in Hertford Street

We had an aerial torpedo take the top of the front of the house off. The blast from it killed seven Irish fellows who lived with a family opposite us. They were sitting in the hall on a bench and they were still in that position when they found them. Also, a young girl was blown on top of the Palladium Cinema roof. The blast blew all her clothes off, except her dress. She was injured, but not badly, just a nervous wreck for months afterwards.[60]

I was helping my Dad on the rescue squad and I remember not hearing the All Clear. The tram lines were sticking up in the middle of the road. One tram was blown over a house into a back garden in Eagle Street and never broke a window on the tram, but the house had a direct hit. We had no water in the house so we had to boil the water from the rainwater butt for drinking. There were no ambulances at all and Courtaulds was on fire from top to bottom. [50]

Directing a fire engine

It was my first day back on leave from the Army and I thought I would make my way to the Canal Tavern in Leicester Causeway, to see some of the lads, when suddenly I heard this noise above. I thought, blimey, there must be a thousand planes up there, when suddenly I was blown to the ground. A crater the width of the road was twenty yards away.

I thought I could make my way home, which was the Humber Hotel. My Dad was manager there then. I got into White Street, when a warden said, "Come on, son, get down the shelter for a while."

I stopped there for a couple of hours, then decided to get home. I'd walked a few yards when a fire engine pulled up and asked me the way to the Humber works. The driver said sit with him, and off we went, but every street we went along we could not make it because of the craters in the road. We went backwards and forwards, but could not get to the Humber works. So I said cheerio, all the best. I went up St George's Road and over the iron bridge to the Humber Hotel. When I walked in, they were all down the cellar, singing and drinking.

My Mum said, "Where've you been, Nobby?"

I told them about the fire engine and they said I must have called in a few pubs on my way home.[57]

Inferno of burning rubble

It was a very cold night but as bright as day, with a hunter's moon. With all the fires raging and all the activity going on, you didn't feel any cold or anything. Some lost their nerve and ended up in mental institutions. There was an incident when a pump crew arrived from Walsall. We saw it get to the end of Friars Road, and then there was one blinding flash. The whole pump, crew and everything, had gone, vanished. They had had a direct hit from a 500 lbs bomb. It went through between the vehicles. All we found later were bits of gumboot and a few mangled tin hats.

We went down to a shelter just off Cheylesmore, in Greyfriars Park [Green?], where there were known to be about ninety people. They were all dead. A bomb had fallen on the entrance and all we got out of it were bodies. The effect of it hit you days later, and you started to think, 'It could have been me'. Those poor so-and-so's who went into a shelter thinking they would be safe.

We got almost to the centre of the town around ten o'clock and Owen Owen was on fire from end to end. There was a turntable ladder with one fireman on the top. Another high explosive came, hit the building, and the blast went up. You saw the top of the ladder bend. The fireman pitched straight into the centre of the fire. That's the last that was seen of the fireman from the top of the ladder.

Records say there were 650 killed [the source of this figure is not clear; 506 rearranged? See below] in the 14/15 November blitz, but I would rather think it would be in thousands — a couple of thousand. A lot of people were not accounted for — they were not at home — they must just have been blasted to smithereens.[105]

Several other witnesses also feel the final death figure of 506, quoted by the Medical Officer of Health and Director of Emergency Medical Services in his report on the blitz to the Emergency Committee must be grossly inadequate. It is only the figure for those who reached the mortuary and were officially "dealt with". How many more were left buried, blown to pieces or taken by ambulance directly to hospitals out of the city? From the frequent accounts by members of the air raid services, of bodies being destroyed, we must assume at least several hundred, perhaps another five hundred, were thus unaccounted for. Other accounts mention a number of shelters in the city centre being sealed off, as they were so badly bombed no one could have survived inside them. It is especially difficult to estimate the final death toll because of all the workers from other towns in the city who would not have relations to inquire after them, plus the confusion of the mass evacuation from the city during the days after the raid. I would think that at least a thousand died, but not as many as two thousand.

This is still a very small figure for a city of 250,000 laid to waste, but can be explained by the bombing being concentrated in certain areas. Although every area suffered damage, the city centre, Foleshill, Hillfields, and Stoke suffered especially harshly. There was a huge nightly exodus from the city or to friends who lived in the periphery of the city. Furthermore, the evacuation of children, women with babies and the disabled from the inner city, and the presence of huge underground shelters which, on the whole, proved safe, meant a great many lives were saved.

Memory recalls the team who were valiantly trying to subdue a raging inferno when the flames of the burning building were leaping like fiery pinnacles into the night sky to such a height that the men and their auxiliary pump equipment were dwarfed to proportions so puny as to appear almost ridiculous......

There was a whine, a scream as the bomb fell. It exploded and, when the dust blew away and the debris settled, there, in the light of the fire, was a huge crater, no more. Men and machine had been hurtled into the midst of the burning building and the fire they had sought to subdue had become their funeral pyre......

As hour succeeded hour through the long and tortuous night, tragedy mounted upon tragedy, the death roll grew and maimed and mutilated men, women and children were given succour. The dead were removed to mortuaries and these places, prepared in all solemnity beforehand to receive the few, were soon to prove all too small to accommodate the bodies which were being brought in the whole night through, and for many days afterwards.

There they lay, stark and stiff, waiting burial like so many warriors after a battle, but a high heeled shoe peeping from beneath a blanket, a curly golden ringlet of hair with the neatly tied bow still in place, a protruding sleeve of a bus conductor's tunic, these and other signs showed that these were not military casualties, but civilian dead.

What of the maimed, but living? What of those rendered homeless, whose numbers increased as the night wore on? On every road leading from the burning city there were streams of refugees seeking the safety of the nearby countryside, some still in their night attire. Every farmhouse and barn for miles around sheltered its complement of men, women and children who had left the apparently doomed city. As they trudged wearily along country lanes, or lay within their newly found shelter of barn or hayloft, they could hear overhead the drone of the German raiding planes coming and going unceasingly on their merciless errand of destruction. They could hear the whine and crash of bombs falling and all around the sky was lit with a lurid glow from the burning city behind them.[43]

Lest we forget

As Phyllis Clark reminds us, let us not forget:

Friends who simply drowned in their rubble-blocked air raid shelter; friends just blown into the walls of their house; bulldozers digging non-stop and finding an old man shielding the bodies of three small children.

Some wardens were blown up and a man came collecting the pieces of human material. There was a piece hanging on a nail outside our back.*[98]*

"Was this really a military target?"

Even the German attackers were awed by the magnitude of that great fire blazing below. At six thousand feet, Oberfeldwebel Werner Handorf could feel his nostrils prickle as the smell of the burning city penetrated even into the cockpit of his Junkers 88. Hans Fruehauf, a veteran of the London raids, stared down at the sea of flames in horror.

"The usual cheers that greeted a direct hit stuck in our throats," he remembers. "The crew just gazed down at the flames in silence. Was this really a military target, we all asked ourselves......"

Sing a Song of Suffering

Despite every effort which was made to check the effects of raiding planes, the Nazi pilots remained in almost undisputed command of the air. Mobile anti-aircraft guns were rushed to all parts of the city to augment the barrage as the raid progressed.

Among the points from which they operated were Broadgate and Pool Meadow, but it was of no avail. So completely did the raiders control the situation that they were able to shoot down the barrage balloons, at least four of which came down in flames, and carry out semi-dive bombing attacks over the city.[93]

One hundred and eleven out of the one hundred and eighty principal factories sustained some damage and particularly badly hit were the Daimler factory at Radford, GEC in Whitefriars Street, and British Thompson Houston in Alma Street. Even more damaging, electricity, gas, telephone, transport and water services were all severely disrupted.[85]

Below is a list of the aiming points which were issued to some of the German squadrons, each squadron having a special target of a key factory or major service installation:

Squadron	Target
Letirgeschwader 1	The Standard Motor Company and Coventry Radiator and Press Company
Kampfgruppe 27	The Alvis aero engine works
Kampfgruppe 51	The British Piston Ring Company
Kampfgruppe 55	The Daimler works
Kampfgruppe 606	The gas holder in Hill Street.[28]

The Daimler

14 November 1940:   Coventry's first blitz. Total number of HEs on the factory impossible to record. Considerable damage to Foundry by bombs, and to the Boulton Paul Shop by bombs and land mine. Many small fires reported; those of a major character occuring in the Body Shop, Boulton Paul Shop, Tool Room, Test Shop and Scout Shop. All were dealt with without outside help, the latter being the most difficult, due to loss of water. Several minor, but luckily no major, casualties. Many unexploded and delayed action bombs were found on inspection and later dealt with by the BD [Bomb Disposal] Squads.[5]

The fire at the Daimler works at Radford, a suburb of Coventry, was not only the biggest single fire the city endured during the raids, but was also one of the largest factory fires in the country. Certainly, few others approached it in the intensity of bombardment to which it was subjected. It has been reliably computed by experts that between a hundred and thirty and a hundred and fifty high explosives, five land mines, nine oil bombs, seventeen delayed action bombs and between two thousand five hundred and three thousand incendiaries, including the explosive type, were dropped. The high explosives ranged from small bombs of 110 lbs to at least one of 3,300 lbs, the first recorded occasion on which a bomb of such heavy calibre was dropped on Britain. It was a delayed action bomb and its tail fin alone was about four feet in length. About fifteen of the factory's forty-odd acres were destroyed or severely damaged by high explosive and fire……

One of the first loads of incendiaries dropped in the raid hit the factory and numerous pin-points of fire from incendiary bombs dotted the main road, as far as the eye could see. The Chief Officer of the works' brigade wondered anxiously how many had fallen on or through the factory roofs, but most incipient fires they did start were put out by works personnel, or else the bombs burnt themselves out on the concrete floors.

The first call was to the Gun Turret Shop, which fortunately was isolated from the main buildings. With the raid continuing, there was immediately another call to the other end of the factory by the main gates where the office block and drawing offices were blazing fiercely. The arrival of an oil bomb on the block added fuel to the flames, which a sharp wind drove along the line of shops. Planes began to stoke up the fire with high explosives and incendiaries and soon other shops were ablaze. These were about forty feet high and some were about four hundred yards long. Wire netting had been placed beneath the glass on the roof as a protection from flying splinters. This trapped many incendiaries and soon the roofs were blazing beyond hope of their being put out.

The fire from the office block spread to the experimental shop adjoining.

The works brigade was just getting it under control when the hydrants failed, the borehole pump having been put out of action due to failure of the town electricity supply. The nearest big supply was the canal which ran parrallel to the works across the sports field and was some six hundred yards away. The firemen were just resigning themselves to the loss of the shop when the hydrants came on again for a few minutes, just long enough for the fire to be put out. Then, after their failure, it was a case of doing whatever was possible amid the rain of bombs.

Meanwhile, AFS [Auxiliary Fire Service] crews had arrived, but had not been able to get the fire fighting effectively organised before the street hydrants went as well. It was some time before the first relay from the canal at the electricity works, about a quarter of a mile down the road from the main gate, began to operate. Hose was contantly being punctured by bomb splinters and these particular lines from the electricity works had to be replaced three times. Then a pile of hose that had been delivered outside the main gates was riddled with splinters from a bomb that fell on the opposite side of the road.

While this was going on reinforcements began to arrive, some of which were sent to the canalside between Cash's and Courtaulds' factories, abutting onto the Daimler recreation ground which ran alongside the factory. One of the reinforcement crews, from Dudley, had just arrived at the main entrance when an HE fell, killing four of the crew of five and blasting the trailer pump into the wall across a small garden with such force that it hung there, a shapeless mass of metal.

A heavy pump sent to Cash's was put to work at the canal bridge there but, owing to a faulty gland, would not lift the water which was twenty feet below. This pump was sent to another factory yard at the Standard Motor Company and used at the canal there, where the lift was only a few feet. To replace the faulty pump, two major trailer pumps were used and twin lines of hose taken across the sports ground and over the railway footbridge towards the main entrance.

When a replacement heavy pump arrived this was also set into the canal at Cash's yard and a hose lorry laid more hose lines to the rear of the Daimler factory to cut off the spread of fire. Both lorry and hose were badly damaged by falling incendiaries and new lengths had to be put in. This relay was later augmented by two more major pumps from the factory works brigade.

The first jets had not been in operation long before two very shaken firemen reported that their mate had been seriously injured. An HE had dropped nearby and blown off part of his face. Miraculously, the other two had escaped. Then, to add to the difficulties, an incendiary bomb fell on the intermediary pump in the relay, severing the electric wiring and putting it out of action.

Shortly after this, when a good water supply had been obtained, a high explosive bomb blocked the entrance to Cash's works, severing the hose lines and putting one of the trailer pumps out of action. A shower of incendiaries followed the bomb, starting five fires among the looms and other inflammable material in Cash's factory.

These fires, which were either side of the lane running to the canal, put the fire-fighters in jeopardy and gravely threatened to cut off their line of retreat. Seven jets were quickly brought into action from the assembled pumps and three of the fires were speedily extinguished. The fourth fire, among some looms, was then concentrated upon and that too put out.

The fire-fighters had just withdrawn when a further shower of incendiaries once again set it alight, and again it was extinguished. By this time the fifth fire, in a two storey block of offices and workshops, was well alight but being held in check by works crews.

When it had been put out, the Daimler fire was again concentrated on, but little could be done to save the buildings, already blazing furiously. There had been an hour's lull while the planes went to Birmingham and good use was made of this respite. When the raiders returned just after midnight they attacked the Daimler works with renewed ferocity and fires were continually enlarged. Eventually, however, further spread was limited and dawn found the fire-fighters in control. The sudden silence that followed the end of the raid was almost as unbearable as the raid itself and, when the men had time to think about themselves, they realised how utterly exhausted they were after a night of terrible pounding. During the final attack one member of the Daimler works brigade received severe injuries from an HE and died a few hours later in hospital in Warwick.[5]

Smith's Stamping works

The middle of November brought devastation to the works at Ribble Road. The company's railway siding received five heavy bombs and the blast stripped the roofs off many of the buildings and damaged the walls. Incendiary bombs set fire to the heat treatment shop and this was burned out. Damage was done to electric motors, hammers, stores, and many items of equipment. Supplies of gas, water and electricity were cut off. There were casualties among the workmen and many of their homes were destroyed.[96]

The Alvis

I was living in Holyhead Road at the time. At night I was attached to the 108D Post, which is by the gas works in Hill Street. On the night of the blitz I'd been down the shelters in Bablake School to see that they were all right and I was on my way round to Lamb Street where there were some more shelters, when somebody said the Alvis had been hit.

I went around by Norfolk Street, as this was the best way of approaching the factory, and up through Barras Lane and down Holyhead

Road, as far as I could get.

It was really ablaze. You couldn't do anything about it, you'd just got to leave it. But there were several people standing outside trying to do little bits with buckets and sand. It was hopeless, but they were trying to stop the fire spreading to the houses. That was their main job. But there was no water, of course. They said that the night shift had got out.

That was at about a quarter to eight, or perhaps a bit later. After I had gone round I went back to the shelters in Bablake School and, of course, that was where it got hit. I was lucky to get out. During the night I kept popping back [to the Alvis], but it was still ablaze. [–] was one of the firemen at the time. I'd heard that he'd been injured trying to fight the fire. He'd been blown from the road onto the railway bank. He's still alive today. I've never asked him; I believe he's got a false eye, actually, or his eye doesn't move much; but he was very badly injured, scarred, and everything.[70]

Courtaulds (British Nylon Spinners)

Key Point Intelligence Officer,
Midland Regional Office,
Civic House,
156, Great Charles Street,
Birmingham 3

Dear Sir,

We are in receipt of your letter of the 25 February and, as requested, give below for record purposes, a short note of the damage which occured to this factory:
1. Damage occured on the night of 14/15 November 1940 to our premises at above address [Foleshill Road] as a result of enemy action, and was due to explosive and incendiary bombs.

One explosive bomb fractured a concrete roof and pierced two floors, and came to rest on the ground floor. It did not explode, but the casing was ripped open, presumably by its passage through the roof and floors. Apart from holes in the floors, minor damage was done to spinning machinery.

A number of incendiaries pierced slate and glass roofs, but no major outbreak of fire occured. Structural and other damage was of a minor character.

An explosive bomb pierced the slate roof and caused minor structural damage.

A Claim Form has been filled in for "Immovable Property" £1,491 10s 0d and "Other Than Immovable" £339 17s 4d.

Repairs practically completed. [This is on 27 February, 1941.]

Electricity, gas, water and steam services were interrupted by damage elsewhere in the city.

2. As the factory was in course of erection, production was not affected, but the effect on the construction programme was a delay of three to four weeks.

3. There were no casualties on the site.

Yours faithfully,
for British Nylon Spinners Ltd,
General Manager [24]

A Courtauld's fireman injured

As a voluntary member of a textile works' fire brigade, [he was Safety and ARP Officer at Courtaulds' main works on Foleshill Road] I was directed to one of many fires within the works complex. A colleague turned on the water, leaving me alone with a powerful hosepipe in a building seemingly the size of a couple of tennis courts. I was not having much success containing the many small fires started by a cluster of incendiary bombs falling on and through the single storey roof.

A near missile explosion; something penetrating my leg above the knee, making me a stretcher case for hospital, my fire fighting brought to an end.

I was loaded into a small van. Two very brave men started a nerve wracking ride to the city hospital. The journey, no more than five minutes from a normal start to finish, seemed endless, with diversions caused by bomb craters, houses on fire and debris blocking the streets. One observation still lingers in my mind. After passing two churches and a chapel on fire, the streets of Coventry were as close as anyone could get to having a first-hand view of hell.

As I was carried to hospital, I thought it very appropriate to being dumped "out of the frying pan into the fire". Directly overhead was a perfect square of marker flares. The city hospital, already burning in parts, was within that square. The casualty hall was full of injured people. Some had walked in or, like myself, been assisted there. After receiving a wound-probing and an anti-tetanus injection, I was carried to join many more stretcher cases on the floor of a long corridor.

The early hours brought some respite, with the easing off in the intensity of bombing. Finally, the drone of bomber engines ceased, soon to be replaced with a sequence of dive-bombing planes. Each plane carried two bombs which, on release, made a screaming noise on the way down. One heard each plane dive and the two bombs falling, but no indication of the target. This bombing continued until 7 am and was, for breath-holding suspense, the worst part of the twelve hour blitz. The complete silence after the last bomb explosion was as uncanny as the mystery of our survival.[100]

The Triumph works

Triumph became a busy unit, mass producing the resurrected 350cc single cylinder version of their discarded range and, in addition, the fifty special 3TW machines were made and assembled. These were packed in their cases and were on the loading deck of our Despatch Department on the night of the big Coventry blitz. They were destroyed, together with the factory and most of its contents.

There was no question of making fifty replacement machines because the Triumph works had been completely detroyed overnight and all was gone. The factory was a write off and our immediate job was to get back to a situation, somehow or somewhere, which would enable us to produce once more. We were left with a smouldering shell and no records.[68]

Cash's, Kingfield Road

At the factory we had had, for many years, an efficient volunteer fire brigade. This proved invaluable in this period of danger, under the successive leadership of Elijah Bucknall (until he joined the Army), Tom Filer and Frank Wallace, the latter having also captained the brigade in 1939 when the war organisation was built up. Mr Harris was assigned the responsibility for general ARP measures, Mr Farndon subsequently acting as ARP Controller. We had two Climax trailer pumps, one large and one small, which drew water from the canal and were capable of directing powerful jets to any part of the buildings.

In addition to the brigade, a number of fire watchers were on duty each night, the fire watching party including tenants resident on the premises. A well trained first aid party was provided by the women and girls, who were not only ready to render assistance in the event of casualties, but also supplied the fire watchers with excellent meals; their energy and enthusiasm never flagged and their services throughout were of great value.

For eleven hours the attack continued, each wave of bombers being succeeded by another at short intervals throughout the night. Our own roof spotters had a front row view of this tremendous spectacle, the vapour trails of the enemy being distinctly seen in the clear sky. Such guns as were available fired throughout the night, but with little effect and, towards the end, the gunfire became weak and spasmodic.

Kingfield was destined to suffer considerable damage. High explosive and incendiary bombs fell all around and it was not long before the houses on the canal bank and the Long Shop above sustained a direct hit. The south end of N° 4 Shop and the houses below, eight in number, were completely wrecked. Another hit by an HE bomb demolished the north end of N°3 Shop and four houses below. Incendiary bombs fell on the Men's Dining Room and the Harness Store in the factory yard, both being gutted, although the efforts of our fire brigade prevented the fire from spreading. A parachute mine which exploded between Kingfield and the Daimler works caused much additional damage to roofs and windows and, when daylight came, it seemed that there was hardly an unbroken pane of glass or a roof that was not stripped of most of its tiles.

During this long ordeal, while there were no actual fires at Kingfield, one of our trailer pump crews, under T Baggott, was called upon by the City Controller to render help in the Priory Street district. Fires were raging in this district, in many cases unchecked, especially during the latter part of the night when the water supply failed owing to bomb damage to the water mains. In this locality alone the Cathedral, the Triumph works adjoining Pool Meadow and the Stevengraph (woven label) works were all totally destroyed. Our pump crew rendered valuable assistance from 8 pm to 5 am, when they returned to Kingfield.[6]

Central Control Shelter, the Humber

Bill Hancock was in the Central Control Shelter at the Humber works. He had just left the toilet at the end of the shelter and returned to his desk when he heard a bomb dropping:

It was a five hundred pounder and it struck the spot where I had been standing. It blasted out the whole end of the shelter and flung us all towards the stairs. I think the door saved our lives, as it took the blast and cushioned it into the stairway.

I was picked up unconscious, covered with dust and rubble, at the bottom of the stairs at the other end of the shelter from where I had been sitting. How long I had been there I am not certain, but I came round in an old building under the stairs of the canteen where I had been carried and thought to be dead. At this time, I had apparently not been recognised.

However, I staggered up and went to see what was left of Central Control, now all in the dark. It was about five o'clock in the morning and I saw some of the ARP and firemen still looking down the bomb hole. Thinking [-] was still down there, I tried to go down to find him, but I was restrained, and eventually I was escorted to the next shelter, which was untouched.

In his report on the raid to the Air Ministry, he named several people who showed bravery that night. Of Mr Albert Bird, he said:

I sent him into the town at the height of the raid to contact the Coventry Fire Chief, as we were running short of water and all the telephone wires were cut.

Of George Collier, his Fire Brigade Chief, for his bravery in attacking a fire at a vulnerable spot:

I witnessed him at the top of a ladder with flames all around, directing a hose right down into the flames.

George Collier received the George Medal and Albert Bird was mentioned in depatches. Of himself, he recalls that:

The Rootes brothers must have mentioned me, as I was awarded the MBE.[59]

Churchill Components

I was an eighteen-year-old lathe operator working for a man named Churchill. No, not the famous prime minister, but every inch a leader himself. His business was aircraft engine parts, hence the firm was called Churchill Components Ltd. I must admit, I used to envy him when he and his family came round to check on production. He seemed blessed with everything: money; lovely wife and family; film star looks; courage (RAF Squadron Leader flying Hurricanes); every boy's dream!

His factory was in Gosford Street, next door to the Fox and Vivien. Across the road was Nuffield Mechanisations (the DHSS building now), churning out Bofors guns, and next to them was Coventry Swaging Co. The last named was destined to be devastated on the night of the full moon, 14 November. The Luftwaffe set it ablaze and throughout the night continually stoked it up. We were working over till eight o'clock that night as usual thinking, when the Alert sounded at seven o'clock, that we might put another half hour in before we went home.

We were stuck there for eleven hours and it put me off fireworks for a long time. Although we came through that ordeal OK, our gallant employer was later to lose his life leading his Hurricanes on a sortie from Malta.[123]

Most key Coventry factories had their own fire-fighting service, rescue party and first aid party. There follow the reports of several of these rescue parties.

Alfred Herbert's Rescue Party

Dear Sir,

We refer to your letter of 3 October asking that you shall be advised of acts of gallantry by members of our organisation working on Air Ministry contracts. Although we are actually under the Control Department of the Ministry of Supply, all our papers on this subject have been destroyed and we are, therefore, approaching you in the hope that, if you are not able to deal with this matter, you will pass it on to the Ministry of Supply department concerned.

The acts of gallantry we wish to bring to your notice occured on the night of the 14/15 November when there was a most intense air raid on Coventry. They are as follows:

Eddie Leonard Hunt,
Chief Officer, Alfred Herbert's fire brigade:
He took a fire crew and engine to the Coventry Ordnance works at 7.50 pm and did not return until [?] am. During this period he assisted the city brigade in fighting a very bad fire whilst high explosives were dropping round them. This officer also took a fire crew and engine out during a previous raid, when he was wounded by falling glass.

Arthur Ward,
Assistant ARP Controller:
Whilst in charge of the rescue gang, he took them to rescue people trapped under burning houses in Lythalls Lane. By his example and courage, he kept his gang at work during the most trying circumstances.

George Mathew Brownless,
Member, Alfred Herbert's fire brigade:
A crew and trailer pump were sent for to deal with a fire in Lythalls Lane, where Ward was engaged. This was in the charge of Engineer Brownless, who carried on in spite of heavy explosive bombs dropping round him, and eventually his hand was severely injured by a flying piece of shell. By his coolness, he inspired everybody to continue keeping the fire in check, so that Ward's rescue gang could get the people out.

William Moody Simpson,
Third Officer, Alfred Herbert's fire brigade:
When he [Brownless] was injured, his place was taken by Third Officer Simpson who, during the whole of the raid period, gave a very cool and brave service.

Walter Ronald Selby,
Fireman, Alfred Herbert's fire brigade:
Fireman Ronald Selby was out with his squad fighting the fire in Lythalls Lane when he was injured in the pelvis by a flying piece of wood. In great pain, he was brought back to the Alfred Herbert Control Room. Later, when all telephones were cut and a doctor was wanted for a man who had been shot in the lung and also [after overhearing that it was vital] to advise the City Control that the AH [Alfred Herbert] organisation was in grave trouble, Selby......went out and crawled to Holmsdale Road Police Station, which was able to put a message through, just before the wires were cut. High explosives were falling the whole time Selby did the double journey.

Robert Charles Griffin,
Member, Home Guard:

Griffin was acting as a roof spotter during the raid. He stuck to his post during the whole time, until the fire station close by was completely demolished.

> Yours faithfully,
> for Alfred Herbert Limited,
> A H Lloyd,
> Director of Works and Design.[122]

Activities of works ARP units during air raids: 12 October — 15 November

Albion Drop Forgings Co Ltd

During the raids which occured in the latter part of October, the works ARP services rendered assistance in extinguishing incendiary bombs in streets adjoining this company's works.

Alvis Limited

During the whole of the above period, sections of this firm's ARP services were standing by, ready for city calls, but it was not until 14 November 1940 that a summons for assistance was received from the city authorities. On the night of 14 November 1940, although all personnel of this firm were heavily engaged in their own premises, a trailer pump together with a crew was dispatched to assist at the RAF Depot, Sandy Lane, where they remained for a period of fourteen hours, before being relieved.

Armstrong Siddeley Motors Ltd

From 13 October 1940 to 14 November 1940, the ARP organisations of this firm on eleven occasions rendered assistance in extinguishing fires to adjoining property (dwelling houses and industrial) and on two occasions rendered assistance in the rescue of persons trapped in damaged properties. Two first aid squads have been supplied to assist the city, from Gulson Road First Aid Post.

Brett's Stamping Co Ltd

On the night of 19 October 1940, the ARP units of this firm assisted in dealing with incendiary bombs falling in the neighbourhood of the works.   On the

93

The still smoking devastation in Broadgate the morning after the blitz

night of 14/15 November, two large fires and nine incendiaries were effectively dealt with by the works fire brigade, in addition to which a burst gas main outside the works was damped down.

British Thompson Houston Co Ltd

During this period there were seventeen occasions on which this company's fire fighting organisation rendered assistance in fighting fires, two of which were of a major nature. In the course of these duties, five of the firm's firemen were seriously injured, and one fireman fatally injured. Throughout this period, the air raid shelters under the Read Street factory of this firm were utilised by the general public, persons using the shelter during this period varying from two hundred to one thousand. Many of them were attended to......by the Works Nurse and the works first aid personnel.

Daimler Co Ltd

On the night of 16 October a gas main was fired and the works fire brigade kept this fire in check, thereby assisting the gas department to cut the supply. On the night of 14 November, although several calls were received by this firm from outside for help, these calls unfortunately could not be responded to, owing to the firm's organisation being fully occupied attending to the fires and damage at their own works.

Daimler Nº 1 Engine Factory

Although the works ARP units of this firm were not officially called upon by the city authorities, these units were active in an unofficial capacity in many parts of the city. On the night of 12 October 1940, the rescue and repair parties gave assistance in Wallace Road and this party worked hard all through the night rescuing several people who had been trapped. On the night of 14 November, assistance was rendered to families whose homes had been damaged and the works shelters were placed at the disposal of these people and other civilians. On two occasions, the works fire brigade assisted industrial undertakings (Daimler Co Ltd and Courtaulds Ltd) in keeping fires under control which had occured at the works of these two firms.

Dunlop Rim and Wheel Co Ltd

Auxiliary fire pumps manned by members of the works fire brigade, at the request of the City Fire Station, were sent to Lamb Street, Coventry, where they were engaged for a period of six hours and they also assisted in extinguishing a fire at Motor Panels Ltd.

The General Electric Co Ltd

On forty-three occasions the fire brigade of this company has assisted in extinguishing fires and incendiary bombs at industrial and private property, crews operating from Stoke, Spon Street, Whitefriars, [Lower] Ford Street, and Queen Victoria Road works. This works fire brigade was particularly active on the night of 14 November 1940, when thirteen fires were attended by the works fire brigade, six of which were of a major nature, five pumps operating in various parts of the city. On three occasions prior to 14 November 1940, and also on that particular night, the rescue squad of this firm rendered assistance in rescuing injured people from bombed property. Shelter has been provided and first aid given where necessary to bombed out people and others at all works, six to eight hundred being sheltered at Spon Street works alone each night during this period. The first aid station and trained staff at the main works have operated throughout, dealing with casualties in the Stoke area.

Alfred Herbert Ltd

On seven occasions during the above period, calls were received by the works fire brigade of this firm, and assistance was rendered to industrial and private

95

property. In addition to this, assistance was also rendered on four occasions by the rescue and demolition squad of this firm, in rescuing persons trapped in damaged property. On the night of 14 November 1940, the first aid nursing services of this firm attended to injured civilians.

Mechanisations and Aero Ltd

On nineteen occasions the works ARP units have rendered assistance in extinguishing fires at industrial and other property, including (on 12 October 1940) Gulson Road Hospital. This works fire brigade was very active in fire fighting on the night of 14 November 1940, when it assisted in extinguishing eight different fires, one of which was at the Coventry and Warwickshire Hospital. Assistance was also rendered in the evacuation of patient casualties from the Gulson Road Hospital during the air raid on 14 November 1940. On many occasions this firm has acted as fire watcher for the city and passed on information to the Central Fire Station. The first aid parties have also rendered assistance, particularly on the night of 14 November 1940.[122]

Many more firms' ARP services were involved on that devastating night, as they had been throughout October. Morris Motors' fire brigade was called out ten times, particularly for a fire at the Binley Road Goods Yard. Action was seen by fire brigades and rescue squads at Reynold Chain, the Standard Motor Company, Sterling Metals, George Wilson Gas Meters Company, Charlesworth Bodies (1931) Ltd, Rotherham and Sons, Singer Motors, Smith's Stamping Works, and Courtaulds. At Rootes Securities, assistance was given to fight the fires at the Humber works and first aid personnel helped in the demolished wards of the Isolation Hospital. The Rover Company reported that, on 14 November, its ARP units treated patients and took them to hospital in the works ambulances, which then rendered assistance to the devastated hospitals.

Typical of many acts of sustained heroism that night by members of the factory emergency services, Nurse Marjorie Eileen Perkins, of Pattison and Hobourn Ltd, was recommended for the George Medal for her selfless service on 14 November. It is fitting to end this chapter with her citation. It read as follows:

On the night of 14 November 1940, Miss Marjorie Eileen Perkins, employed as a Works Nurse by Messrs Pattison and Hobourn Ltd, Cash's Lane, Coventry, was in charge of the works surgery. Normally, she would have gone off duty at 10 pm but, owing to the very intensive and sustained air attack which Coventry experienced that night, she remained on duty until 9 am the following day.

During the whole period she rendered excellent service to casualties at the works, in the nearby streets, and at the public shelter at Messrs O'Brien's offices a short distance away, despite the fact that bombs were constantly falling all around. On two occasions, Nurse Perkins was flung across the surgery by blast, the first time being injured internally and the second time being rendered unconscious. After recovering consciousness, although in considerable pain, she carried on, dealing with further casualties, both at the works and outside, cheering and attending to those workpeople who could not be moved and visiting the shelters and encouraging everyone to remain calm. Throughout the night she did her work with utter disregard for her own personal safety; her courage and devotion to the injured under the most trying circumstances were outstanding. Since that time, she has had to remain under the care of her own doctor.

Controller's remarks:
The gallantry outlined above has been corroborated and I recommend the award of the George Medal,
S A Hector,
Chief Constable and ARP Controller

I recommend that Miss Marjorie Eileen Perkins should be considered for the award of the George Medal for her courage and devotion to duty during the Coventry raid.
[Lord] Dudley[99]

Nurse Perkins received her George Medal a few months later.

Crescendo of Fire

Air raid log: 14/15 November 1940

Friday 15 November

6.50   Bramwell and Entwistle signing off (after White [the All Clear]).

Note: The night has been one of a very intensive raid of between 400 to 500 instances.   Twenty land mines, HEs and UBs very large quantity, incendiaries in huge numbers (eleven hours continuous intensive bombing). The main feature has been the **lack of water for fire fighting.** The Cathedral, Jordan Well, High Street, Broadgate, Palace Yard and Bayley Lane have suffered mainly fire damage **(Could have been avoided and some of these buildings saved had an adequate water supply been available?)** Finally, N° 1 Post Tower requires checking to ascertain whether now safe after tonight's hit.

Note: Log-book taken away for safety and will return later.

Left.
           E S Bramwell[23]

As the raid went on, hour after hour, the city's essential services broke down. Fire hydrants were buried under the rubble.   Water mains were shattered by bombs.   Those who were still attempting to fight the blaze had to drag water by hand from the river and the canal.   Rugby's fire brigade arrived, but had to stand by helplessly and watch the city burn.[7]

By 8 pm the Central Fire Station had charted two hundred and forty fires, many of them out of control; and thirty minutes later volunteer firemen drafted in from Rugby found the city centre's water mains fractured.   By 9.30 pm the telephones were out; Coventry was cut off from the outside world. Slowly, the defenders were acknowledging defeat.   At 11 pm the Provost, Richard Howard, and his fire watchers abandoned the battle to save St Michael's Cathedral. From the doorway of St Mary's Police Station they listened, sick at heart, to the steady drip-drip of molten lead until the great steel girders spanning the nave, glowing red hot, "tugged the walls and pillars from their foundations like so many Samsons"......

For every Civil Defence worker, it was the most frustrating night they ever knew. Ambulance driver Katie Fensom never got within sight of the city's two hospitals, the Coventry and Warwickshire and Gulson Road, all evening; high explosives had cratered the roads like a lunar landscape, cutting off all access. Auxiliary Fireman John Bowles, who brought a fire engine eighteen miles from Birmingham, was checked by a policeman who counselled, "You may as well go back, mate; you can't even get in".

By midnight many men were as resigned to die as rescue worker Albert Fearn. He told himself, "This is the end. We'll be dead lucky if we see the sun again."

A few found relief in action. In the sixteenth century courtyard of Bond's Hospital, a home for aged men, old Edwin Walsh was up all night smothering incendiaries with sand. Told to lie down, he demurred stoutly; he had lain down for no man all his life and he didn't intend to break the habit at ninety years of age......

Soon after midnight, word came to St Mary's Police Station. A shelter under Smith's Furnishing Store had been hit and fourteen people were trapped. Police Constable Wilfred Burchett was one of eight men making up a volunteer party to rescue them but, at length, after an hour's digging, he and two others were dispatched to enlist more help.

The errand saved their lives. Minutes later, a hurtling bomb wiped out the five men who had remained.[21]

Unprecedented bombardment

The Chief Fire Officer reported on the devastating extent of the bombing and the numerous obstacles the fire service faced during that terrible night:

The intensity of the bombardment increased and all reports indicated that the attack was of an unprecedented nature for a provincial town. Incendiary bombs, explosive incendiaries, oil bombs, HE of all calibres, parachute mines and flares were all being used. This "all type" bombardment continued throughout the night whereas, in previous raids, incendiaries had been used only in the early stages, followed by high explosive. Many large factories, stores and serious risks were involved, and initial calls for assistance indicated that most of the fires had secured a good hold in the first instance. Outside aid was arriving but, owing to the swiftness of developments, not quickly enough to provide the maximum first attendance of pumps required at most outbreaks.

To add to the difficulty of operation, fires were started in the roof of the Headquarters Station, after the second of which it became necessary to abandon the Control Room. Water from these fires caused the switchboard to become "alive" and by 8 pm all the lines from here were out of order. The main lighting failed and the emergency lighting was badly affected.

Reports of water shortage from the town supply began to come in and, at 9.10 pm, three heavy relay units were requested, with the remainder of the third assistance. Telephonic communication had now become difficult and indistinct. Static water supplies were already in use and, as the town water supply position became worse, long relay lines were introduced. The prepared dams in the River Sherbourne were used at each of the ten points and at no time did this supply fail, as fortunately there was a very good flow in the river on that night.

Swimming and ornamental pools which had been earmarked were brought into full operation, as well as factory reservoirs. In some cases, these latter had only been installed after much persuasion. The pre-arranged relaying schemes operated very satisfactorily, although blocked streets and debris necessitated diversions and subsequent collapsing buildings called for new lines by different routes. Supplies from the canal were also utilised until it was hit by HE at a point at which a storm water culvert passed underneath. The sudden and complete loss of water in this important section of the canal near the centre of the city was not explained until daylight.

At 8.47 pm the remainder of the telephones (except a private line to the Control Centre) were out of order for outgoing calls, and only two operated spasmodically for incoming calls. When incoming calls were received from reliable sources on these lines, the opportunity was taken to relay outgoing calls elsewhere; in this connection a line was kept open for a time to the Leamington Fire Brigade and many calls were transmitted by that route......

At 11.15 pm forty more pumps were asked for, also the assistance of professional officers to replace one killed and two injured of our own.

By now the position was critical...... Outside assistance was held up by road blockages at considerable distances from the Central Fire Station and had to be marshalled and diverted. This presented almost insuperable difficulties. All available messengers and spare men were engaged on piloting and guiding out-of-town crews, but new road blockages were so frequent that traversible routes could only be found by actual trial. Even so, it was impossible for the great majority of crews to report to our stations.

In the circumstances, of course, guides were instructed to take them straight to fires. In addition, many out-of-town crews found fires and got to work on their own initiative. The messenger system was used to its full extent but it will be realised that we had a tremendous task in attempting to pilot every assisting crew or convoy via innumerable diversions. The whole time there was a feeling of uncertainty regarding the safe arrival of messengers. Not until each one returned to report could any satisfaction be felt.

The fires in the centre of the city eventually combined to make a single incident and, owing to the congested nature of property, there was no alternative but to concentrate on preventing the spread of fire. In spite of attacks upon pump crews working from static supplies (which probably reflected the moonlight and fire glare) and repeated destruction of relay lines, the spread of the fire was checked with a large measure of success.

The early loss of the services of three regular officers and several regular men soon began to make itself felt and meant a tremendous strain on those left. The direction of operations called for strategy and resource, for which there were few previous standards to act as guidance. Fatigued and under continual bombardment, they worked incessantly, without relief or refreshment. Time out of number fires were extinguished and buildings practically saved, only for the buildings to be partly or wholly destroyed by fire or HE due to renewed attacks, under the eyes of the crews making up equipment......

In many cases, after fires had been dealt with, pumps had to be abandoned owing to being hemmed in by debris and wrecked buildings. Detachable light pumps were, of course, recovered where possible but this could not be done with large units.

In no known cases were sprinkler systems responsible for extinguishing fires, although many buildings destroyed were so equipped.

Particular care had been taken to distribute stores, but all three places were hit and practically everything destroyed. Greater distribution would appear desirable, or to accept the inconvenience of stores situated outside the city. Our records were duplicated but, similarly, both offices were damaged and records lost.

Large stores and shops would be well advised to remove black-out arrangements at closing time, as fires are liable to remain hidden until they have secured a good hold. Even when they do make themselves apparent the extent of the fire cannot be quickly appreciated......

The number of fires recorded up to the breakdown of communications was two hundred and four. In addition, during this time, many fires were not reported, some of these being dealt with by police, wardens, other services, and civilians. The numerous fires which occured after the breakdown of telephones were not, of course, recorded, but must number several hundreds. A number of personnel sustained fatal injuries. Up to the time of reporting:

Coventry Fire Brigade	1
Coventry Auxiliary Fire Brigade	7
Coventry works brigades	12
Assisting brigades and AFS	6
	26 R.I.P.

The number of personnel injured must have been at least two hundred. Of these, thirty-four are known to have been serious.

Two brigade tenders, nine towing vehicles and seven Home Office pumps were destroyed as a result of enemy action; the brigade turntable and several pumps and towing vehicles were damaged.

W H Cartwright
Chief Fire Officer[27]

The Coventry Fire Brigade had established a system of auxiliary fire stations, fire patrols and fire posts throughout the city, in six zones. For example, Foleshill and Bell Green zone had five auxiliary fire stations, seven fire patrols and fifteen fire posts. It had one heavy, four medium and seven light pumps. The zone's total crew numbered ninety-eight, plus five telephone operators, seventeen spare men, and four "professional personnel".

In all, Coventry had twenty auxiliary fire stations, forty fire patrols, and a hundred and three fire posts, with some five heavy, fifteen medium and forty light pumps.

During the raid, the city received assistance from a hundred and eighty fire pumps from other areas, plus three turntable ladders, ten heavy pumps, ten hose laying lorries and twelve mobile water carriers, together with all their crews, plus some two hundred and fifty relief firemen from London [one account says two hundred] and others from as far away as Manchester, Leeds and Bristol.

More and more help was requested from fire fighting services outside the city. Never before had there been such a continuous hail of incendiary bombs and high explosives, hour after hour! At 8.55 pm the London Fire Control had arranged for twenty-five pumps to be sent to Stoke-on-Trent from Manchester, in case they were needed to help cope with the Coventry fires. At 11.50 pm, mobile water carriers, hose lorries and heavy pumps were sent to Coventry, and an additional twenty pumps and crews were ordered to report to the city. To relieve the exhausted Coventry firemen, the London Fire Control arranged for two hundred and fifty firemen to be sent by bus to the city to act as reliefs.

At 2 am over two hundred fires were reported to be burning fiercely. The fires were not brought under control until 12.50 pm the next day. Even then, many continued to burn, although they did not spread further.[28]

Central Fire Station hit

I was in the Control Room. It was very well organised at first, until the water situation became very serious. Crews weren't able to go on fighting fires because they didn't have the water with which to do it. So, then it became quite chaotic.

There was a shelter at the back of the yard of the fire brigade and everyone eventually went in there, with the exception of the Divisional Officer and one other lady; Mrs Hampton, I think her name was. We were all ordered into the shelter, but this one lady stayed.

Some of the fire engines carried a water supply. They relied on the canal to a great extent, but also, in the roads, there are standpipes to which the fire brigade could attach its hoses......

Too many fires, yes, because it went on until the early hours of the morning...... They had a lot of casualties, because firemen were blown over streets and over houses. When they were fighting fires on factories, the glass roofs gave way and they fell through. There were all sorts of horrific injuries, because there weren't just fire bombs, there were high explosive bombs as well, which were destroying all the buildings within the city. So, obviously, if the firemen were there, they were injured very badly. April [1941 — when there were two more raids of comparable intensity] was not quite so severe, not quite so concentrated, but it was bad.

We had a fire patrol in each street and the churches had their own fire fighting teams with stirrup pumps and buckets.

The fire station was hit during the November blitz. I'd been sent upstairs to get something and the office was near the tower of the fire station. While I was looking in the cupboard, right by the side of the tower, I heard a terrible noise and fell flat on my face on the floor. Then I discovered afterwards that the tower had been hit by a bomb.

At the time I didn't realise it, so when I came to get out of the office, I couldn't see the staircase. It was so covered with rubble and there was smoke and dirt and dust in the air. But I could hear my husband's voice calling me from down below and they guided me down the stairs, because they realised that I was up there. But I was perfectly all right.[112]

Water Board HQ "washed out"

It was fortunate that on 14 November the conditions throughout your committee's undertaking were normal, all previous air raid damage having been made good, and the quantity of water stored in your committee's reservoirs was 21.3 million gallons......

On the night of 14/15 November, your committee's normal ARP organisation reported in full on the initial warning, and I am pleased to be able to report that, throughout the whole of the night, the personnel on duty responded to all calls upon them, even when these calls involved personal danger.

During the most intensive periods of bombing, all incendiary bombs which fell within the waterworks area at Spon End were promptly dealt with and a fire which broke out in the upper floor at Spon End Depot was fought and got under control, saving the depot buildings from almost certain destruction. During the period when the fire at the depot buildings was receiving attention, the Alvis works immediately adjacent and out-buildings of the Coventry Chain works were blazing fiercely and the area heavily bombed.

The Departmental ARP Headquarters at Spon End Depot were literally "washed out" and temporary headquarters were established at the first aid post, which was previously the manager's house. Although these temporary headquarters received damage, they were manned until further telephone communication with Central Control could not be established.

Subsequently, action was taken from Spon End and other immediate action stations entirely [dependent] upon conditions and, during the early hours of 15 November, members of the turncocks' section penetrated into the centre of the town in an attempt to detect and isolate damaged trunk mains, which were indicated by our inability to maintain pressures.

Following the failure of the mains electricity supply at Spon End and Whitley, the diesel driven alternators at these stations were set to work and were operated continuously. In spite of the very severe conditions at Spon End, the personnel at the Pumping Station and in the Diesel Generating Station attended to their work with the utmost calmness and efficiency.[125]

Motorcycle Messenger Service

The sirens went at 7.15 pm. Charlie and Ted had just gone down to the Three Spires to fetch some beer. Ted had been busy all afternoon digging a hole and erecting his mother's shelter. We didn't go down the shelter straight away, but waited for them to come back. They came at about 7.45 pm. Charlie went to the ARP post and we all went down the shelter and took our supper. The gun barrage was terrific. There were some good fires going already. Ted was not due on duty until 10 pm, so he sat with us in the shelter until 8.30 pm, when he decided, as it appeared a bad raid, he must go on duty and not wait for 10 pm.

The first incendiaries hit the Alvis and it blazed furiously, then the Rialto Cinema was hit and on fire. This was at 7.15 pm, immediately after the sirens. Ted went on duty down Allesley Old Road. A bomb had fallen on a little church by Spon End arches, so he went along The Butts and St Patricks Road, which were clear then. There were fires all around him in Much Park Street. Two factories near to the police garage were well alight. Incendiaries fell on the Mechanics Shop, but these were quickly dealt with.

The Market Hall, the city centre, and the Cathedral were burning well. The people were quickly got out of the shelters under the Market Hall. PCs Kite and Fox went to fetch the Chief Constable. Foulger was in the brewery cellar and Ted stood outside the office waiting for the telephone calls. The telephone rang. An escort was needed to meet a rescue party from Wolverhampton at the city boundary, consisting of five vehicles, and escort them to George Eliot Road — on the opposite side of the city — where fifteen people were buried under demolished houses. This took between thirty and forty-five minutes. Whilst passing through the city centre on solo motorcycle, Ted was blown from his motorbike in Jordan Well by the blast from bombs that killed his best friend and colleague, PC [–]. Luckily, he escaped injury and was able to continue his journey to meet the rescue party. He arrived at the police garage at 1.30 am.

He had to go back to the garage via Police Headquarters, as he had to report to the control room. Another rescue party was waiting, but, as the situation was getting intense, the Chief decided it was not worth risking his men's lives sending them out, so Ted went back to the garage. To get back, he had to ride his motorcycle on the pavement outside the Council House, as all the shops on the opposite side of the road were ablaze. As it was, he was scorched by the intense heat. He turned down Little Park Street. Bushills was blazing fiercely and he had to ride in the centre of the road and blind through it. The heat was intense. It was impossible to reach the top of the street as the flames were meeting across the road and the roadway was blocked by piles of bricks and girders. If it hadn't been for Cheylesmore car park, he would have been trapped, but he was able to ride across the car park into Cheylesmore. Two more fires at the old Swift Skating Rink were blazing well. From there, to Much Park Street, to the police garage, there were other fires. In fact, the whole of this area and the city centre was a blazing inferno.

When Ted got into Much Park Street he found the roadway completely blocked by house bricks and rubble from houses and a small shop which had been demolished by a direct hit. A man standing there who Ted called upon to help him carry his motorcycle over the pile of bricks, told him that two elderly women who lived at the shop were buried in the cellar under where the shop had stood. Ted went back to the garage and obtained assistance and went back to get the old ladies out. Both were found still sitting in chairs they had occupied before the direct hit, having dropped into the cellar in their chairs, and being covered by wooden timbers and bricks.

When uncovered, one was found to be uninjured, apart from bruises, but the other lady was dead. During the course of uncovering them, Ted and the other helpers conversed with the one alive, reassuring her. She kept replying that she was all right, but there was a lot of pressure on her chest.[103]

Rescue squads active all night

Every rescue squad had to make a detailed report of its activities during the night of the blitz. It is evident from the detail of the reports that they were well organised and efficiently run, with a network of rescue posts established across the city. As squads arrived from as far away as Manchester, they were directed to particular areas or incidents, where many of them were still working when the dawn finally arrived.

There follows a selection of excerpts, with house numbers deleted to protect the grieved. Unfortunately, in the first account, many of the street names are inaccurate, but the general progress of the party is still clear:

At approximately 7.30 pm we [the Coventry Motor Spares rescue squad] received a call to proceed to Treherne Road, off Jubilee Crescent, Radford, to search for three persons suspected of being trapped in a house. The course of our journey took us along Gulson Road, Much Park Street and Broadgate. There were a large number of bombs falling, one of which we actually saw fall into Owen Owen's shop. Fires were just beginning to take hold, the majority of the incendiaries then having been dropped.

On account of fire parties, etc, we were unable to negotiate our way through Broadgate, but turned down [?] Street, and Jesson [?] Street. At this time, no great damage had been done in any of the streets.

In Leicester Street [Row?] we found a bomb crater which already had a car in it, around which we proceeded and made a straight run along Radford by Lydgate Road and Grangemouth Avenue [Road]. We arrived at Treherne Road just as large quantities of land mines were being dropped. Persons, we discovered from the local warden, who had been in the houses had been evacuated.

I then suggested that we split up into crews as best we could among the remaining houses in the street, which we did. Judging from the debris, I should say that land mines had caused the damage. At this point, a special constable came and told me that there were persons trapped in an Anderson shelter which had received a direct hit behind the [public house]. I left certain numbers of my squad at Treherne Road and told them to deal with anything that came along and I then proceeded with two other members to the [public house]. One of the squad had to shoot a dog that was in a bad condition in Treherne Road. At the [public house] we removed three persons alive from the above mentioned Anderson shelter, a middle-aged woman, a girl and a small child suffering from shock. A number of people had been killed outright.

We then proceeded to Control, the rest of the squad having arrived from Treherne Road and, on our way back, more high explosive bombs were being dropped and also further landmines, although these appeared to be diminishing in quantity. The time was then approximately 9 pm.

On the way back we stopped at Radford Church [St George's? It had its church hall destroyed, which was acting as a rest centre, and it could well be that that he is refering to: or perhaps it was St Nicholas', which was destroyed in one blitz] which a land mine had totally demolished. We found three persons, one able to walk, one a sitting casualty, both suffering from shock, and one with injured legs. We decided to use the stretchers we had and subsequently loaded them into an ambulance which turned up a quarter of an hour later.

In the stokehold we found three girls, one slightly injured and all of them suffering from shock. One of them we sent off in the ambulance accompanied by her friend, the other remaining on the scene.

We then proceeded to Control via the Birmingham Road [Holyhead Road] which was then obstructed under the bridge, with the Alvis blazing heartily. We returned along the side of the railway through the Coundon Goods Yard and back to Control. Mr Naylor then instructed us that there were persons injured or trapped in a celler at [–] Smithford Street, whither we proceeded, through the city centre and along Smithford Street at 10 pm.

The conditions there were very bad. We searched the premises of half a dozen shops on either side of [–], but could find no one whatever about. When we returned to our lorry, a bomb had damaged a house on the left, bending the front axle of our lorry and removing its nearside front tyre.

We again proceeded to Control, which advised us that it was the Co-operative Society's premises where the cellar was assumed to have been inhabited by trapped persons. We returned again, finding that during our absence a crater had been made in Smithford Street. The Co-operative Society was then burned out. To effect an entrance to the cellar was difficult, but when this had been done we found it to be devoid of any persons.

I returned with one of my squad to Control to receive further instructions and we were then sent to the Gaumont Picture Theatre. We found upon enquiry that there was nothing for us to do, whereupon we returned once more to Control and received instructions to go to The Bull Yard, at the rear of the Three Tuns Hotel.

Our road taking us past Bushills, we found that this was completely burned out. We went along past the back of Holbrooks [the firm], whose bridge had practically burned out. The ARP store was just catching alight from Holbrooks.

Arriving at The Bull Yard, we worked there for the remainder of the night, removing persons who were trapped. I cannot remember the exact number that we got out, but I think it was in the region of a dozen being alive and suffering from only slight injuries and shock, in most cases. We removed two dead persons who were obstructing our passage, in the removal of the live ones.[36]

At our first incident we found there were four people still alive. Somewhere under the tangled mass of beams, bricks and rubble were men and women. A bomb had fallen nearby and the blast against the side wall of the house had brought the whole building down. There was such a terrible heap of rubble that we could marvel if a snake survived, let alone people.

With great care, based on our experience of earlier raids, we searched, probed and shouted. Then we listened — hard. The layout of the house was studied by looking at the neighbouring ones which were still standing. We tried to locate the likely position of the staircase, the place where people usually sheltered.

After our first, careful survey, we started the actual rescue. Everything had to be done slowly and with great caution. Just one false move and we could bring down even more of the building. Foot by foot, an eighteen inch tunnel was slowly driven through the debris......

The first man to go in worked full length, passing out the rubble he cleared

Members of a rescue squad at Sandy Lane, near the Daimler works

and drawing up the tools he needed by a line. Other tunnels were started from other directions. Yet we still needed to take great care. One mistake and another rescue squad would be needed to dig us out!

Almost there! Just one more yard, and surely that was the side of the staircase. We had already managed to contact the people who were trapped there. One person was badly injured, pinned underneath a girder.

Just one hour later, and four more people who never expected to escape alive had been brought to safety from the ruins.[28]

Stechford Rescue Squad

Arrived Coventry 10.35 pm, Thursday 14 November 1940
Left Coventry 11.30 am, Friday 15 November 1940

Impossible to get to Control HQ without half an hour or more delay. Foreman went on foot to Police HQ; instructions received for [–] Forfield Road, Radford; searched house, but could not find any casualties. We then searched seven other houses in the same block which were damaged — no one in any of the houses. Wardens confirmed that all were in shelters and safe.

Could not get back to Control HQ, but found other incidents as bombing continued. A house in Barkers Butts Lane was reported by a civilian to have two people trapped; we released them from under the stairs and they were quite safe and sound.

[–] Moseley Avenue — demolished. Three people were reported by the warden to be in the house. Miss [–] and a soldier were found under the debris — slight injuries and taken to hospital. Mr [–] was later recovered dead.

A report came from a soldier that three people were trapped in houses demolished in Mill Street [Bablake]; we recovered a man from [–]. He was slightly injured and taken to hospital in a private car, as a sitting up patient. We continued the search next door for a mother and daughter; after working here for some time, the son came along and said that they may have gone to a shelter. The squad continued working while we made enquiries at public shelters. Mother and daughter were then found to have moved to a shelter and were safe.

We reported to Police HQ at 8 am, 15 November and received instructions to proceed to [–] Grosvenor Road, where four people were reported trapped in cellar. We worked with the Kidderminster Rescue Squad here. They had already found a boy alive; later we recovered the mother and two daughters:

Mother: Mrs [–] — recovered injured, taken to hospital
Son — recovered injured, taken to hospital
Daughter — recovered dead
Daughter — recovered dead

General remarks:

Glass on the roads caused two punctures and, as we only had one spare, we had to run with one flat tyre. A dispatch rider went back to depot at Stechford with instructions for another vehicle; this eventually reached us in good order.

The emergency rations which were sent out by the Depot Superintendent by private car duly reached us and were very welcome.

Debris and craters caused considerable delay in getting around.

From our experience in getting to Control Headquarters at Coventry, it would appear advisable, in the case of regional calls, for incoming parties to be met at the main road boundaries with instructions and guides.[122]

Coventry Gauge and Tool Rescue Squad

The Salvage and Rescue Squad under its Officer in Charge, Mr Clarke, rendered valued service to the city's rescue organisation by its services at Jordan Well. A tobacconist's and furniture dealer's shops were still burning nearby. Three females and one child, all fatal, were recovered. Similarly, eight other bodies, all badly burned. Following the report that seven persons were buried beneath the remains of the [–] Hotel, a careful search was made by the squad, but the report was not confirmed.

During the recent rescue and salvage work by the squad, one man was very notable for his outstanding service. This man, Jenkyn Shanklyn, of [–] Lime Grove, Tile Hill, stopped at nothing and left no stone unturned to carry out his duties to the end.

There follows the citation for Mr Shanklyn:

Beanfield Avenue —14 November 1940
He dug his way through the debris of two houses near a huge bomb crater and, after an arduous task, found two male bodies, which he dragged out and carried to ambulances. Despite the fact that he was told by the police that no other bodies were under the debris, he searched further, removing bricks from the stairway and there found a female alive. She was conveyed to hospital in an ambulance.

Barracks Square, Old Rover works —16 and 17 November 1940
Mr Shanklyn showed extraordinary courage, working without a break from early morning to late afternoon without food and with only a little whisky. He heaved, with almost superhuman strength, on girders and masonry and himself ploughed through debris and removed eighteen terribly mutilated bodies. Convinced that there were further bodies, he smashed with a sledge-hammer and crowbar at heavy concrete and requested that some steel girders should be burnt through. Amazingly enough, one female was found uncon-

scious and conveyed to hospital. It was found a week later that she was still alive.

Jordan Well, [–] Hotel — 17 to 20 November 1940

Mr Shanklyn was the outstanding figure of the rescue and salvage squads. He had been told by the police that two of their comrades had entered the building to look for a bomb, before the collapse of the building. Mr Shanklyn searched through what he considered to be the passageway and there found two terribly burned remains; these were considered to be the police officers. After a little revival of whisky, Mr Shanklyn re-entered the debris and found later a ten-to-fourteen month old infant, clasped in the body of its dead mother.

These two finds were bad enough, but Shanklyn returned without taking lunch and, whilst his comrades were having refreshments, came from the debris with three females, badly burnt. In the afternoon, Shanklyn returned and discovered in all twelve badly burnt bodies, which he himself removed to safety. Shanklyn stated that he had a sense of persons being in the basement. These were partially filled with debris, but Shanklyn got below the surface and searched all eleven cells and eventually came out with a man's body. He reported that what was believed to be the mother and a fourteen-to-sixteen year old son were still in the basement. Despite slight injuries, he ploughed his way back and brought both mother and son out in turn.

It is stated that, from 16 to 20 November, Shanklyn took no food from his start of work in early morning until late afternoon and was an example to all who worked with him. Following his service, Shanklyn had to receive medical attention for a skin eruption which had broken out all over his body. Shanklyn receives the highest commendation from all his ARP officers.

Mr Shanklyn was very reluctant to give the foregoing information.[122]

Jenkyn Shanklyn received the British Empire Medal for devotion to duty.

Humber Road shelter

Rescue Party depot:	Binley Road
Position of incident:	Humber Road shelter
Instructions:	None. Instructions taken from police
Date:	14 November 1940
Time:	20.00 hours
Action taken:	All rescued
Persons rescued alive:	Four
Dead taken out:	One

On the night of the fourteenth, our first call came by police messenger from Box 25, as our phone was early out of order. This was to proceed to Briton Road immediately. Every man was ready, equipped with lamps, first aid, water, etc.

After a few minutes, it became obvious that the van had no intention of starting, so an immediate conference took place as to what to do. We informed Central Control and asked for instructions or a fresh motor and we were told to proceed to the Humber Road public shelters. Instantly, we men grabbed crowbars, shovels, picks, etc, and went on cycles while the driver took four members in his own car. By this time, the raid was at full intensity and we had to refuse to assist some civilians who appealed to us to help fight a house on fire on the Binley Road. It was here that one of our men was struck on the arm by one of the incendiary bombs which were falling all around, making us feel like being on a stage, owing to the blinding glare and flash. As we jumped off our cycles, we ran to the incident, where we assisted and left in charge of the FAP [First Aid Post] men the five casualties, the last of whom we had to dig from the heavy clay.

Bombs were falling behind us as we went back to the depot and our next call, as by now all telephonic communication had ceased, was to Brompton Road, where again the men ran, walked and cycled to the incident. After accounting for all people there, we were subjected to a particularly heavy bombing, but the men had by now ceased to take any heed of the scream and crash of the night of terror.

Our next call, which came after we had put a batch of various types of incendiaries out after they were dropped around our quarters, was a warden's appeal for help to Bolingbroke Road. There we found a father and daughter trapped by their legs under their iron fireplace, which was blown on them when the house was hit directly. In ten minutes, the man was free and, as we had no tools, an appeal to neighbours soon brought a crowbar and jack, and here I must pay a compliment to the pluck and courage of the young woman who, though in pain, with several tons of masonry crushing her leg, bore up well. After about twenty minutes she was free and, returning a badly bent crowbar to the neighbours, we left them to the FAP men who were working by torchlight in the houses.

We wondered if the dawn would ever come, as now it was 5.30 am and still the raid was as violent as ever. We spent the rest of the blitz waiting further orders in our depot which, though shaken and vibrated, weathered the storm.[122]

Swan Lane Rescue Party

We proceeded to Frederick Bird School. A message came that a boy, believed to be alive, was trapped in the debris. [Many schools had shelters, first aid posts or ARP posts on their premises, explaining the presence of people at Frederick Bird's.]

When we arrived there, we found a woman's body, which we laid ready for removal, and also located a boy's body, which we found to be dead, and also two more trapped and dead.

At that moment, a message came from Mr Stafford to proceed to [-] Mickleton Road, where there were two persons trapped. On arrival, we found the Hereford Squad there, who were removing a woman's body, dead. They did not require our assistance, so we returned to depot and then proceeded back to Frederick Bird School, to find two bodies had been removed from the debris by two Home Guards. We then recovered the boy's body.

Hand written note:
......off Alfall Road, people trapped alive.
Rescued:
One woman alive
One man dead
One girl dead
One child rescued by Manchester Squad.[122]

Harnall Lane Rescue Party

On receiving instructions from the Control Room we proceeded to the [-] Club, Spon Street, Coventry, finding the concert hall demolished. We gathered from the people round about that people were in the cellar at the time of the bombing. This was under the concert hall, which we found to be concrete with a boarded floor on top. Also, the roof of the hall was of a concrete and iron construction. On removing these, we found parts of bodies and whole bodies. While work was proceeding there was a time bomb within three yards of us.

On being told by the military to stop work at the above we then proceeded to Trafalgar Street. [We began knocking] down a chimney breast on two floors and part of the back gable, which was unsafe. This had to be done before we could proceed with our work of rescuing bodies near the fire place which were badly burnt. After this, we received orders that a body had been left in the Club, owing to the time bomb. I should like to point out that we went back, knowing quite well there was a time bomb a few yards away, and later took the bodies to the mortuary with labels on each one.

Bodies taken to mortuary by our van......
    Five from [-] Club
    One from Trafalgar Street.[122]

Lockhurst Lane Rescue Party

Our first call was from Control at 20.55 hours on 14 November to proceed to Houldsworth Avenue [Crescent?], off Nunts Lane. We found wardens and first aid men at the incident, injured people being clear of the debris. After making sure we were not further required, the party returned to the depot, to find ourselves out of touch with Control. Contact was made with wardens from Victory Road and Brookville posts (local districts).

We were next called out by the Victory Road warden to a shop in Lockhurst Lane. The premises being on fire, we had difficulty searching for persons believed trapped. We made an entrance from the rear of the premises to the cellar, finding one man needing medical attention. First aid and an ambulance were fetched from Livingstone Road station for attention and transport.

Our third incident was to assist three persons trapped beneath the debris of two houses in Burnaby Road (near the Pilot Hotel), at the request of the Head Warden of Brookville post.

On leaving this incident, we were called to others in Rollason Road by wardens from the same post. The first incident was at numbers [–,–,–,] and the second at numbers [–,–,], where happily we were unable to find any trace of persons trapped as suspected, the occupants being found in shelters or to have evacuated the premises.

This completed our work for the night.[122]

Birmingham and Rose Road Rescue Parties

The two groups worked very hard and, although not able to rescue any live persons from the wreckage, they were responsible for recovering the bodies of fifteen persons and conveying them to Hill Street mortuary, where they also did good work in assisting the attendant.

They were working from early on the Friday morning and did not leave Coventry till about 4.30 pm, with only a small break for very light refreshment.[122]

Broad Street Rescue Party

On the night of the raid, I arrived at the Leicester Row depot at 10.00 pm to find War Reserve Officer N° 54 asking for men to accompany him to an incident in Springfield Road. I at once made contact with Mr Bingham, Depot Superintendent, who was in charge of the phone and offered to go with the officer if I could get together enough men willing to go with me.

Several men offered their services, but I could not take them all. I picked out six men and drove to Springfield Road to rescue four persons trapped. Four persons were liberated from there and we returned to the depot. Mr Bingham told me there was a call to George Eliot Road. It was 11.15 pm.

As we got on the Foleshill Road at Harnall Lane, an HE dropped behind us and the blast sent the van over the road. The driver, Mr Duffield, showed great courage and skill in holding the van down. He has my greatest praise and thanks for his daring in driving through what I think was hell on earth. We got as far as Bishopsgate Green. We were stopped by a crater in the road. While there, we assisted in rescuing four persons from the property adjoining the AEU Club. All four were rescued alive and sent in a RAF van to a depot somewhere at Gosford Green. Mr A Barnes showed great daring and courage in getting these people out while the building was still falling around them.

We returned to Lincoln Street and made our way by Mortons, which was burning fiercely. We searched three houses in Lincoln Street, but found them clear, so we carried on and managed to get to the incident in George Eliot Road, after dodging a rain of incendiaries on the way. It was 12.30 am.

We proceeded to extricate a woman we found trapped under the stairs, which had collapsed under the weight of the roof. While the men carried on with the work, myself and a Volunteer Reserve named T Johnson searched the adjoining houses, smothering incendiaries. We found two persons under the stairs of a house two doors further on and sent them to O'Brien's shelter in the care of a first aid party which had arrived at George Eliot Road from a Wyken post. We extricated the woman from under the stairs and floors at 4.30 am and left her in the hands of the first aid party. We tried to get back with the van, but could not because the road was blocked both ways, so we abandoned the van and walked back to our depot at Leicester Row, arriving back somewhere close to 5.00 am, where I made contact with Mr Bingham. I have nothing but praise and thanks for the courage these men showed while with me.[122]

There was this one bloke who had been trapped under some wreckage and was obviously seriously hurt. After helping to free him, I draped my coat over him as he gritted his teeth and joked that he hoped he'd be playing football on Saturday. But when we tried to move him, he screamed with agony. Finally, one of the first aid men started to work on his injured leg, cutting away the trouser material. As soon as the cloth parted completely, the man's leg fell apart as though cut by an axe from thigh to ankle.

My coat was eventually returned to me, along with a pound note and a message saying, "Thanks pal, have a drink with me". It proved a pathetic hope, as I learned shortly afterwards that, during an operation to amputate his shattered limb, the man had died.[92]

Dispatch Rider Service

Towards midnight, all telephone communication was out of action and the entire dispatch rider force dispersed over the city.

Ambulances and fire tenders from the outlying districts began to arrive at the city boundaries, where dispatch riders were waiting to pilot them to areas of greatest destruction, using their local knowledge to avoid bomb-cratered streets or roads made impassable by wrecked buildings. George West and his wife, of the Mayoress Club on the Holyhead Road, now the Mountbatten Club, did yeoman service all through the night, serving tea, coffee, or pints of beer to the Home Guard, Civil Defence, police, etc, during lulls in the raid.

Finding his way blocked by bricks and rubble, a dispatch rider began to assist in clearing a way through. Under some timber joists lay the mutilated body of an elderly man, close to death. On his jacket was pinned a row of medal ribbons, and one rescuer spoke in anger, "This poor old man probably went through Mons, Ypres and the Somme without a scratch, and here he is, squashed like a rat in his own home."[103]

'A' Company, Nº 2 Battalion, Home Guard

Night 14/15 November: Following the usual procedure, two NCOs and sixteen men were on duty at the guardroom at Lime Tree Hall and, following the Alert, other men reported at headquarters in Whoberley School. Altogether, between forty and fifty men were available soon after the commencement of the raid.

Although this area did not suffer to any intensity, a fairly large number of HEs, incendiaries and DAs [Delayed Action bombs] were dropped and the men were engaged in dealing with incendiaries, locating DAs, evacuating the population in consequence of the latter, and escorting them to shelters. Guards were placed on streets necessarily closed and the men were actively employed till 5.30 am on Friday the fifteenth. At 4 am a broadcast was dropped just behind Fisher and Ludlow's factory and in the vicinity of the Standard Aero works. Men of this Company, together with a few from the anti-aircraft battery, worked strenuously to put out these bombs. They had extinguished the lot, about a hundred and fifty, in about twenty minutes. This was good work and very probably saved the factories from severe bombing.

From an early hour, I tried repeatedly to get in communication with the police station and zone headquarters, but communications had completely broken down and, as no instructions were forthcoming, I acted on my own initiative.[1]

Of cars and cowpats

Whilst on patrol in Lincroft, we heard a cluster of small bombs coming down on the allotment, and one dropped near the houses but did not explode. On investigation, we found the bomb had buried itself beneath this chap's garage, with an Austin car inside. We advised the bloke to shift it, but he wouldn't go near the thing. By then it had been reported. We were bartering with this lad and offered him £10 for the car if we moved it. He had just about agreed when

116

the bomb disposal crowd arrived and spoiled our business venture by digging up this small 50 lbs bomb.

On another occasion...... the Jerries scattered small incendiary bombs on the rifle fields at Allesley Old Road. Before the explosive caps went off, and having nothing handy like sand or earth [to put them out], the only things we could find were cowpats. They proved the perfect answer, for the soft pat moulded itself round the bomb and the fierce heat from the burning magnesium hardened the pat to a concrete cap which very effectively excluded the air. If ever war returns — and I sincerely hope it never does — I recommend [you] keep a bucket of cowpats on your porch, although I cannot guarantee the same results with an atomic bomb![63]

Home Guards Arthur Butler and Roy Holmes

We grabbed hoses and ran out four lengths to reach some double doors. As we pushed them open, we were met by a blast of hot air. Arthur ran back to the pump to get the water turned on. It came through at full pressure, knocking me off my feet and drenching me from head to foot......

We got out just in time as the roof [of the Daimler] fell in and responded to a fireman who helped us drag the hose and askcd us to direct the jet over the heads of four other fire fighters on the roof, so that the spray might keep their clothing from scorching.

Soon the flames were breaking through the roof. All of a sudden, a huge ball of fire shot into the air and the whole of the roof caved in, dragging the four men with it. The screams of those men frightened the life out of me.

The wall in front of us collapsed inwards, showering us with red hot debris. Behind us in Daimler Road a couple of houses were hit. The blast flung both of us against what was left of the wall and, if it had been two feet lower, we would have been thrown into the inferno.

More detonations followed, one after the other. Men were being tossed about like rag dolls. Arthur yelled, "The fire pump's been hit," and ran. I followed. Debris was still falling and there was a huge crater where the pump had been. On the edge, a lorry lay on its side.

Torn pieces of Auxiliary Fire Service clothing hung from telephone wires and a jacket with only a torso lay in the middle of the road. Steam came from it as the blood cooled and a sleeve complete with hand stuck out of the mound of earth. Thinking a man lay buried, we started to dig with our hands. We found only a severed arm. We gathered together what we could and laid them by the fence. By this time, I began to feel ill, and the look on Arthur's face told the same story. Very little else could be done.

Before we could decide what to do next, more bombs came hurtling down. We just flung ourselves to the ground as each one landed. The detonations came closer and closer......

Thirty yards in front of us the road erupted like a volcano, shock waves hit me and I could hardly breathe. Next, there was an almighty thud behind us. Arthur got to his feet and gave me a kick as he went by, shouting, "Run, you silly bugger, that one hasn't gone off." I jumped to my feet and followed, then, whump! The blast hit me, I hit Arthur, and we both spun across the road and landed in a heap in the gutter, with me on top.

We picked ourselves up and followed a group of firemen and Home Guards onto Radford recreation ground. They were making for a public shelter and hoped to scrounge a cup of tea. By this time, the group were twenty yards in front when, without warning, they disappeared in a sheet of flame. Twenty yards to our left another bomb hit the ground. My head went numb as more bombs hit the houses by Westfield House. I was deafened as debris was flung into the air. I sank to my knees and squeezed my nose, so that my hearing came back.

I looked up. Arthur was running towards where the group of firemen were, yelling as he went, "Stop praying and give me a hand!" A Home Guard sat dazed, with one arm torn off. Groans guided us to two firemen, one with all his limbs missing, the other with his stomach hanging out and no limbs.

Arthur shouted, "There's an ambulance coming up the hill," and ran to stop it.

I wrapped my field dressing around the wound of the Home Guard. Arthur came running back with a young chap. He was a Red Cross cadet and we got him to have a look at the firemen. He shook his head. "Sorry, they're done for." Then he took the Home Guard back to the ambulance.

The moaning of those two men prompted me to seek help from the people in the shelter, but not one came forward. They just turned their heads away.

"There are wounded up there. Won't anyone help?" Still no reply. I got mad and yelled, "You b...... load of cowards, call yourselves men?"

A woman came forward and offered to help and, as we were leaving, I turned and gave them another blast. "You b......s. I hope you can sleep at night!"

As I left the shelter, Arthur returned to say that the badly wounded firemen had passed beyond human aid. It was the first time I had ever seen tears in his eyes.

We gathered what remains we could find and laid them under the trees. Bombs were still screaming down, one hitting the railway line at the end of Daimler Road and others blasting the recreation ground. One hit a shelter lower down Lydgate Hill and muffled screams could be heard, but there was no one in the part that collapsed.

In Lydgate Road a bomb dug a crater in front of a speeding ambulance and, when the dust cleared, the vehicle lay with its bonnet deep in the hole. There seemed to be no one around so, still with thoughts of a cup of tea in mind, we took a short cut through a back garden. More bombs fell, some of them so close that a flying brick struck my steel helmet and a house we had just passed took

Bomb craters and extensive damage in Much Park Street

a direct hit......

[Arthur went off to search for his parents, whilst Roy returned to his family in their shelter.]

On going to the front of the house, I saw flames from a fractured gas main lighting up the street. Neighbours across the road were trapped in their shelter and could not get out because of the flames in front of it. After helping to dig the people out I returned to my family's shelter, but felt uneasy and decided to go and find Arthur.

No one had seen him and, as I searched, the picture was one of tumbling houses and shops, a blazing school [perhaps Radford Primary School], and another hit on an ambulance. I was blown across the road by a blast......

As I got to my feet, an object hit me full in the chest, knocking me backwards. As my head banged on the school boundary wall, I lost consciousness. When

I came to, my head felt as if it was in a vice and all I could see was a red blur. My hand touched something warm and wet, my vision cleared and, on looking closer, I saw part of a human torso. I vomited and crawled away and lay with my head overhanging the gutter. The ambulance lay on the side of the road in a tangled heap and I got to my feet and staggered towards it. The body of a man lay half out of the cab, and he was wearing a Home Guard uniform.

I turned and ran, my legs went weak and I collapsed in the road. Then I crawled over to a garden wall and sat with my back to it. If only I could talk to someone……

I was close to cracking and decided to go home by way of Bede Road. On nearing the top, I heard the scream of a single bomb, the likes of which I'd never heard before — like a train entering a tunnel at full speed. I flung myself flat and waited for an explosion that didn't come, only a great thud as it hit the ground. 'Delayed action,' I thought and ran as fast as my legs would carry me. Turning right into Cheveral Avenue, I fell into a hole that seemed too small for a bomb crater.

My knee touched a metal object that I took to be a gas main, but I stayed put because the hole offered some protection from the enemy bombers. When I realised I was just across the road from a land mine, I bent down to get my helmet. I found I was sitting on a huge bomb, probably one of those nicknamed a Hermann Goering because of its vast girth.

I reached home in record time and, as I entered the shelter, my father looked up and said, "You look as though you need some sleep."[67]

Arthur was just seventeen when he was killed and buried in one of the two mass communal graves at the London Road cemetery. He received a posthumous commendation for his bravery. Roy was only sixteen.

The city crippled, bleeding and broken

Around midnight I ventured cautiously to a city-side exit and looked out to see the sky alight with reflected flame all around and across the city centre. Lower on the horizon, above the line of railway track, the Cathedral spire and the water tower of the Morris factory in Gosford Street were stark in silhouette against a yellow blaze of light that stretched from one limit of vision to the other.

Realisation that the 'top of the town' was being destroyed that night sank in. Apart from the Dorniers and Heinkels dropping load on load of bombs, land mines and fire bombs, the crescendo concluded with dive bombers, flown from France to screech down on a flaming target, defenceless, open to anything which the enemy chose to inflict on it. Guns no longer fired, fire fighters had no water to hold back the flames.

The city was crippled, bleeding and broken.[98]

Caualties flood into hospital

The Coventry and Warwickshire Hospital occupied a large site close to the Royal Ordnance works. Every night it displayed bright red lights in the shape of a cross on its roof. Both factors made it a prime target and it was hit at 8 pm, then again at 8.30 pm. In the course of the raid, numerous direct hits destroyed half of its in-patient accommodation. Some wards were severely damaged by blast and many of the stores, the laundry, staff quarters, workshops and other premises were destroyed by fire.

By midnight, the Coventry and Warwickshire Hospital was without water, sewerage facilities, electricity, blackout curtains and windows. Meanwhile, the ambulances, first aid parties and first aid post workers were in constant danger. The ambulances were exposed to the most intense of the bombing as they made their hazardous journeys to the hospitals, past burning buildings and over cratered roads.

I could hardly believe my eyes. All around the hospital grounds glowed literally hundreds of incendiary bombs, like lights twinkling on a mammoth Christmas tree. Down below I could see the men of the hospital staff running from bomb to bomb, dousing them with buckets of sand. Half a dozen small fires had already started in the hospital buildings; flames were licking through the roof of the laundry and another blaze was going on the roof of the emergency storeroom next door to it. From the roof, the Hospital Superintendant was shouting instructions to the hospital's auxiliary fire crew down below. As we watched, however, flames leapt out of the roof of the main storeroom.

I left them fighting the fires and went down to check up on the reception building where casualties would arrive. Everyone was waiting tensely, but the preparations had been completed smoothly. Voluntary stretcher bearers supplied by the St John Ambulance Corps had laid out wooden trestles ready for the stretchers.

I had just completed my inspection when the real fun started. First, an incendiary fell on the roof of the nurses' home. Fortunately, a workman examining the roof the day before had put his foot through a rotten section and a nurse passing along the top floor corridor happened to look up and see the incendiary perched on the end of the hole. The fire was put out before it could get hold. No sooner had the last nurse left than a heavy explosive crashed into it and exploded on the thick concrete top floor. This was our first direct hit......

About 8.30 pm another shower of incendiaries started fires on the top of the Men's Medical Ward and the Eye Ward. With the other surgeons, the orderlies and the nurses, and even some of the more able patients, I ran across the open space between the main building and these wards and began transferring the patients. The nurses wheeled the beds outside while the rest of us hoisted patients on our shoulders and carried them pickaback across to the main hall. As I reached the door of the main building with the last patient on my back, a bomb screamed down and plunged into the Men's Ward. I saw the whole wall of the building fall slowly outward and crash across the open ground where we'd been a few seconds before.

We put the patients on stretchers and blankets along the main floor corridors, which were already so crowded that I had to tread carefully to get from one end of the hospital to the other. Then the casualties started to come in from outside.

We had made elaborate preparations about classifying the patients as they came in, but they began to arrive so fast that we didn't have time for detailed examinations. All we could do was divide them roughly into resuscitation cases and those requiring immediate surgery. The resuscitation cases were whisked into beds and given electric blankets and oxygen to help them recover from the shock of their wounds. The immediate surgery cases were divided among the theatres. I suppose I did about fifteen operations throughout the night. The other theatres handled about forty.

We couldn't work very rapidly. The majority of cases were of lacerations and injuries to limbs. The complication with bomb lacerations, however, is that you get a small wound on the surface, but extensive disruption underneath. Everything is pulped together. It's no use fixing the surface wound without doing a major cutting job on the inside.

Every few minutes, the theatre shook with the thud of a nearby bomb. About midnight, the electric power went off, but I continued with the operation I was on by the light of two small bulbs run by our own emergency lighting system. Every few minutes the nurses and the anaesthetist threw themselves under the operating table as the bombs roared down. I didn't like to follow them, but every time one whistled uncomfortably close, I instinctively pulled the knife away and ducked sideways.

Up on the top floor of the Gynaecological Ward we had fifteen women whom we couldn't move. They stayed in their beds throughout it all without complaint, although a bomb that smashed the staff quarters next door covered them with glass from the window and plaster from the ceiling. In another wing we had a dozen fracture cases. All night long they lay on their backs, unable to move, hung up on their frames, and watched Jerry planes cruising above the firelit sky through a huge hole that had been blown out of the wall of their ward......

The beds began to fill up quickly. The operating theatres began their tasks. Sometimes, we would have to clear away thick dirt before seeing the patient; they seemed to have been dug out of the ground. We were using emergency supplies and hurricane lamps. The casualties then became a never-ending stream......

About 1 am, the engineer sent up a message that our steam supply had failed. Fortunately, we still had a good supply of steam-sterilised dressings in the drums, and we managed to use sterile solution for the instruments, instead of boiling them.

By this time, the windows in my operating theatre had been blasted out and a bitter cold wind was blowing across the room. It was too cold to uncover patients and too cold to operate, for I was shivering from head to foot. The windows in the second theatre had also been blown out, so we were forced to move into the ground floor theatre, the windows of which were protected from the blast by an outside wall. We decided to take turns doing the operations, but since one theatre could not cope with the large number of cases, we could only take the most urgent ones. When I had a few minutes off between turns, I went along the corridors for a cigarette. It was an amazing scene...... far worse than the descriptions I've heard of the frontline casualty clearing stations of the First World War. Patients were lying head to toe on every inch of space.

The nurses were marvellous. With hurricane lamps and hand torches, they moved about the patients, comforting them and giving them sips of water. Near the entrance lobby, I noticed the Hospital Superintendant. He was kneeling beside the patients lying on the floor and, as I passed along, I could hear a few words of their prayer.

Although we have only four hundred and forty beds, we had two hundred and seventy-five patients in when the raid started and I estimate that at least three hundred more were admitted during the night. New patients were put on the top of the beds, while the old patients sheltered beneath them.

By 4 am, I couldn't keep a steady hand any longer. Then our emergency lighting failed, just as I was in the middle of an operation. We quickly rigged up an automobile headlamp to a battery set and I finished the job. Bombs were still crashing down, and every few minutes hunks of earth and debris crashed against the brick wall outside the theatre. By this time, no one bothered to duck.[119]

They starved me all day Monday and they couldn't operate because we had a raid, so they starved me all day Tuesday, and they couldn't operate on Wednesday, because we had a raid on Tuesday night. So they starved me all day Wednesday and they decided in the end they would have to operate, even though we had another raid that night. So I had my operation on Thursday and that night we had the biggest raid so far. I had to get out of bed and get underneath it.

The nurses' shelter was at the end of our ward and they were dropping incendiaries. We were close to the canal. They [the bombers] could see the light shining on the canal, the moonlight. And we heard all the nurses screaming when they dropped incendiaries on the entrance to their shelter. A bit frightening. Bit frightening [Here she cries]. The worst part was hearing the nurses screaming.[78]

Some of the thousands of extra workmen drafted into the city after the blitz clear up the wreckage of the Coventry and Warwickshire Hospital

I was recovering from an operation in Clews Ward of the Coventry and Warwickshire Hospital. As I lay in bed, I saw the wall opposite breaking up and falling. A doctor and nurse tried to shield me from the falling debris by lying across my bed. They had to evacuate Clews Ward. Soldiers from outside were among those who carried me and the other patients down the old, spiral staircase in our beds. The hospital staff and the soldiers were marvellous. They guided the more helpless patients out of the battered buildings.

I think we were taken to a basement room and I was the first patient to be left there in the dark. I heard a bomb screaming down and I screamed with it. I felt so terrified. A soldier ran back and held me tightly to reassure me.

The room soon became full of beds. An incendiary bomb stuck in the wall opposite our beds, looking exactly like an old-fashioned torch. The worst part was the awful noise, and I remember the blessed relief when the All Clear sounded, and the sudden silence.

As daylight came, we all looked about us, taking stock of the situation, and the ward sister who had stayed on duty all night went off for a few minutes. She came back on duty washed, with shining blonde hair and clean cap, dress and apron and wishing us all good morning, as if nothing out of the ordinary had happened. We were all delighted and cheered and clapped her. I think she was Sister Harris, or Harrison.

I was sent by ambulance to Stratford-on-Avon and put into a geriatric ward, though I was only twenty. At Stratford, the nurses thought I had suffered from burns, but my complexion was marred by nothing more that dust and dirt from the crashing debris. But when they removed my dressing gown, they found a large piece of jagged glass next to my skin, having penetrated bedclothes, nightgown and tightly-bound dressings.[129]

Nurse Gladys Crichton, covered in blood, left the scene of horror in the wards to snatch a hurried breakfast. When she returned, she learned that they had been digging for her.

She had already experienced bomb casualties during earlier air raids and from before the war when the IRA bombed Broadgate. Blackout nights caused casualties from people walking into cars and falling down steps to shelters or into craters. In the nurses' home she lost most of her clothes when shrapnel tore through her wardrobe.

When patients and most of the staff were evacuated from the Coventry and Warwickshire the day after the November blitz, Nurse Crichton was with a group which stayed behind to deal with incoming casualties. They got an open fire going with a pan of boiling water to sterilise the equipment. She remembers the loneliness she felt as the exodus from the city began, some people leaving in cars with mattresses on the roof, others pushing prams with their few belongings.

When the WVS [Women's Voluntary Service] came with hot soup it was like manna from Heaven. She slept on the floor of the X-ray department with the volunteer team, in case the Germans struck again. They had to improvise until the hospital began functioning more normally again.[38]

Gulson Hospital fills with casualties

Bombing every now and then was close. Flares were seen and some of the anti-aircraft shells could be seen going up and then bursting. Several fires were burning by then and an incendiary went through the hospital laundry roof. I tried to get at it, but it seemed to be inaccessible. While there, the whistle of a bomb nearby made me dash under a table and, as it burst, pieces of plaster fell from the ceiling.

Luckily, the incendiary burnt itself out. Patients by this time were crowding in. A quick examination was made and short notes written. The hospital is a two storey building and only the ground floor was being used. The wards filled steadily and the nurses off duty were gradually called in till all but twelve out of forty-eight were working hard.

At the beginning not much was to be done except treat for shock and do first aid dressings. Most of the patients were severely injured. There were compound fractures of all varieties, severe lacerations, burns, etc. Dust and dirt covered all of them. They were very good indeed and hardly a word of complaint was heard, except asking for water. Most seemed to be from private houses in the street, some from shelters. A number died after admission and their places were quickly taken by others.

The downstairs wards were filled about 3 am. A hundred and ten beds and the receiving ward had to be used, the patients remaining on their stretchers. About ninety were here, all close together; like the wounded in *Gone With The Wind*, someone said.

Throughout all this, the hospital was continually shaken by bomb explosions and anti-aircraft fire as the night wore on. The hospital remained intact, and most of the staff got used to it, until not much notice was taken.[15]

Raymond Turner was one of the patients during this hectic night. He had received severe foot and leg injuries and was taken to a first aid post. After having his wounds treated he was put in an ambulance to be whisked to Gulson Hospital. On the way, the ambulance was hit by an incendiary bomb which pierced the roof, killing the patient on the top stretcher and forcing the vehicle into a bomb crater. When he eventually arrived at the hospital it was in darkness, the doctors and nurses wearing miners' helmets and lamps. The wards were in considerable confusion. Mr Turner was overlooked and left on the floor all night, covered only by a travelling rug, until he was finally attended to the next morning.

Of the forty full-time ambulances and eleven from the Hospital Saturday Fund, twenty-six were damaged in this single night. Two ambulance garages were destroyed, and one of the six mobile units was damaged. The Emergency Medical Service store in Crow Lane was gutted by fire with a total loss of contents and the emergency mortuary in Hill Street sustained damage to its roof and lost its water supply. Foleshill Baths and Barkers Butts School first aid posts were destroyed by high explosives.

In the former [Foleshill, or Livingstone Road Baths], a parachute mine completely demolished the swimming baths which formed the post, two ambulances and a Corporation bus. A driver and sectional officer were injured.

In spite of this occurence and without electricity, water or gas, the personnel of the post, many of them young girl volunteers, carried on with hand torches and dealt with a large number of casualties without showing any signs of fear or panic.

In the latter post, while over two hundred casualties were being attended to, a land mine exploded nearby, blowing all the windows out of the post. All the patients were moved into the corridors and cloakrooms and the work of dressing the wounds continued. Owing to the presence of two delayed action bombs close by, orders were received to evacuate the patients to N°s 5 and 7 posts, which evacuation was completed by 04.00 hours, and within half an hour a further HE fell on the post, completely demolishing the nurses' quarters.[31]

There were other first aid posts at Gulson Road Clinic, Centaur Road School, Green Lane School, Allesley School, Whoberley School, Wyken School, and in King Street. One mobile unit alone dealt with seventy-five casualties. One doctor in one first aid post dealt with a hundred and eighty cases, at least, many patients returning home without being recorded. Pressure on the mortuaries was so great that, in one hour, sixty bodies were brought in. About half were so badly mutilated they were unidentifiable.

Amongst the many awards and commendations for service to duty that night, Hubert Jones received the George Medal, as did Barham Percy and Marjorie Perkins. Arthur Massey was awarded a CBE for his work with the medical services and, for his bomb disposal work throughout this time, Corporal W Hone was awarded the George Medal. The list of awards during 1940 to 1941, as recorded in the newspapers of the time, number scores of Coventrians, many for George Medals and one, Brandon Cross, for the George Cross. A F Campbell was also awarded the George Cross in 1946.

During the last months of 1940 and early months of 1941, the following were awarded George Medals:

Thomas Lee,	Frederick Mason
P S Brookes	Albert Griffiths
H L Brooke	Dr Henry Gregg
Joyce Burton	Albert Searn
F Walker	W J Wilkinson

The following were awarded MBEs:

Pearl Hyde	Michael McNicholas
Aileen Costigan	Charles Codling
W F Saxon	John Wilkins
William Williams	Thomas Wilkinson

Hubert Jones and Barham Percy received their medals for the same piece of action. Jones (48 years old) was Head Warden of Post 403B in Stoke and Barham (aged 32) was Deputy Head Warden. Their citation, as reported in the *Midland Daily Telegraph*, reads as follows, for:

Valiant conduct on the night of 14/15 November when, for eleven hours, the

Nazi Air Force rained bombs on Coventry in the most murderous attack of the war. The two men were associated together in an incident when three houses were completely demolished and several persons were buried beneath the debris......

They worked in furious spells of ten minutes each, so difficult and trying was the task, digging under the debris with their hands. The roof of the house was hanging over them, likely to collapse at any moment. The debris had to be propped up by timber, and by crawling under this, Jones and Barham were able to rescue a girl alive.

Then another bomb exploded nearby, causing the debris to collapse, Barham being buried and subsequently rescued by Jones at considerable risk.

Even then, the two men were not beaten. Within a few minutes, they resumed their own rescue work and later succeeded in getting another person out alive. In the course of these operations, and in order to reach a cavity, Barham was suspended head downwards for a considerable period while Jones held his heels.

The two men worked without a break under the most difficult and dangerous conditions, and were completely exhausted by their efforts.[94]

Policemen killed

Police killed: 2 Police Constables
                               1 Police War Reservist
                               4 Special Constables
                               2 teenage Police Messengers
                                       R Lowrie (16)
                                       B West (17).[124]

Eleven Air Raid Wardens, including one woman, also lost their lives that night. May they rest in peace.

128

Dawn Requiem

The BBC was severely criticised for the following "depressing" broadcast, but, in retrospect, we can be thankful for its uncompromising honesty:

When dawn broke the following morning, it was drizzling and there was a mist over the town. Men and women began to crawl out of their shelters to look for their friends and survey the ruins of their city. They could hardly recognise it. It was impossible to see where the central streets we knew so well had been. That Friday morning we were surprised when we heard that a building had *not* been hit. It seemed hopeless with our homes, shops, places of work and so much of our lovely old city in ruins.[18]

Friday 15 November

Fires still burning, unchecked all round the city centre, craters and rubble in the streets.

The devastation is indescribable.

Service personnel make their way slowly over the debris.

No one speaks.

My personal feeling is one of sadness.

Then, I recall the starlings trilling a few notes of song as Entwistle and I left the Council House this morning. Did the heat of the fires make the bird think it was Spring, or could this be a message of hope for the future?[23]

It was about six o'clock in the morning. The air was heavy with dust and fumes. You could smell gas everywhere, also a smell of smouldering wood and rag.

I went along the Binley Road, meaning to go down Gosford Street, but Gosford Street had had many DA [Delayed Action] bombs and was closed to the public. I went down Paynes Lane and followed along with other people down East Street.

East Street was absolutely awful. Most of the houses in one part were merely shells and the window frames had flames leaping up and down. Glass was falling everywhere. Children were running around in their pyjamas and slippers. Their houses having been bombed, they had no more clothes.

Some people were lying on blankets, as they had been dug out of their homes and were waiting for ambulances to take them to hospital. Everywhere, folks could be heard crying.

I carried on until I reached Grandma's, seeing the same unhappiness

129

wherever I went. My Grandma, Pop and Darkie were OK, thank Heaven. Darkie, God bless her, had stood as well as any human and was now escorting Popa around the Cathedral.[121]

After ten years memories fade and grow dim. Can anyone now recapture and record the horror, or conjure up again the fitful glare of a burning city, the drifting smoke, the debris of demolished buildings, derelict vehicles and grim-visaged, mentally stunned people picking their way through the ruins on that November morning?[43]

One eye-witness, Madge Faulkney, watched in stoney silence, numbed as soldiers searched the streets, "picking up bits of arms and legs and putting them in potato sacks, as if they were working in a harvest field".[92]

Although it was November, people arriving at the edge of the city next day noticed that the air was as warm as if it were Spring. It also remained almost dark at midday because of the fog, a black fog that hung over the streets and obscured the sky. It was a fog of soot particles, the residue of a town centre which had been incinerated.

For two days, the city was stunned. Everyone knew someone who was a victim or homeless. There were no shops open. There was no water. There was no telephone...... With communications knocked out, people were leaving as best they could, for all roads were impassable for a mile from the city centre.

Coventry had no suburbs, unlike London, in which to find a hospital roof where the services were working, so people trekked out to the surrounding villages and the open fields. The rest centres in the town had been over-whelmed and [many] had been bomb damaged. Like the water mains, the drainage system was damaged. Soon there were notices urging, "Boil all drinking water and milk!" as a precaution against typhoid.[43]

When I emerged it was a bit shattering because I'd been sent to get something for one of the officers [at the fire brigade's Central Control] and the place where I had to go was through Broadgate. I had to climb over piles of debris and rubble because the whole of Broadgate was shattered. I had an awful job to get down to the place I was sent to. All the shops had gone and there were still firemen damping down and people trying to sort out the damage and see if people were buried underneath the rubble. So it was quite shattering when I came out into the daylight and saw the result of the night before......

There was a great feeling of comradeship. There was a certain amount of looting by one section of the community, but everybody else helped everyone else. There was a great feeling of togetherness.[112]

We were all taken outside on the grass verges in front of the hospital. It was very cold and you could see the frost on the trees and grass, but nobody seemed to feel it. We were all too amazed to see the destruction and to know we were still alive.

As the morning went on, the ambulance came and we were put in. After what seemed an endless journey, we found ourselves in Stratford-on-Avon. We all had to have a good scrub when we got there, as we were unrecognisable, hair matted with oil, cuts all dried in blood, all our possessions lost, gas mask, ration books, identity cards, and all.[119]

Lonely, solitary figures

I was standing at 9.30 am on the morning of the 15 November, a small, lonely figure in the middle of Broadgate. I had been on first aid night duty at N° 2 Rootes factory in Aldermoor Lane all during the fateful bombing. The factory had been lucky, with only one small bomb penetrating the roof, causing little damage and no casualties.

Unable to sleep, I decided to walk to Broadgate, little realising the extent of the tremendous damage and destruction. I was unchallenged as I stood among the devastation. Small groups of firemen, ARP personnel, police and the Army stood around, gazing helplessly at the useless, twisted fire hoses. The water and electricity mains had been shattered.

A double decker bus was a smouldering shell and, behind it, the proud new Owen Owen store was now just four blackened walls. Even the cellars below ground level could be seen filled with fallen masonry and hot girders. Smoke was still coming from smouldering beams of the Coventry Cathedral, a new chapter of courage and witness to be written in its proud history. Miraculously, the spire still stood, pointing to the sky above, from where ruthless destruction had come only hours before. Well known shops, Maypole Dairy, Samuels, Burtons, Ashleys, Slingby, Lyons, had mostly disappeared or were badly damaged. The National Provincial Bank seemed to be the only undamaged building, standing out defiantly white among the blackened surroundings.[115]

We climbed from our shelter like ghosts. Everywhere lay desolation and fire. Neighbours took us into their home for breakfast.

After being fed, I started digging in the rubble. My mother had forty pounds in a tin box. I eventually found it, but suddenly I felt someone watching me. I looked round and there stood my father, his face ashen. He said, "Are you all that's left, Joe?"

I was that filled with emotion, for a moment I could not speak. Then I managed to cry out that they were all having breakfast in a neighbour's house.

131

The tears streamed down his face. He clasped me tightly. We knelt there amongst the rubble, and thanked God for our deliverance.[82]

Struggling just to exist

As dawn broke, we emerged to find a pall of smoke over the entire city. We found the way back to our street, making many detours owing to delayed action bombs, fires and unsafe buildings, but we could not enter our area because a land mine was still intact. We found the families of the rest of the children; they had all survived and had been aware that Myrtle and Clive were with us, as a message had got through to them.

Eventually, Dad and I got to my fiance's family and they offered us a roof over our heads until we could return home. There was no water, gas or electricity, precious little food, stores were destroyed, and it took months before even the essentials of life were available. Coventry was like a ghost town; nearly every house was damaged in some way, whilst living was just a matter of merely 'existing'.

We had been requested not to visit the city unless it was really vital, as the damaged buildings were being blown up by the Army, so it was several weeks before I saw the damage in the city centre. I walked between Holy Trinity and the Cathedral. The organ was being played in Holy Trinity and the tracery of the empty windows of the Cathedral was silhouetted against a blue sky. This sight touched a chord within me and tears ran down my cheeks as I thought of all the suffering I had witnessed. [58]

Smoking ruins of city centre

The morning after the November raid, we all had to walk to work. My father walked as far as the GEC in Uxbridge Avenue. When he left me to go to work I carried on along to Gosford Green where we were directed along Paynes Lane, as Gosford Street was blocked, along Berry Street, King William Street, down Primrose Hill Street and into the still smoking city. Everyone was walking about dazed, hose pipes still lying across roads, through an unrecognisable Broadgate and into work.

I believe the telegraph department on the top floor had been on fire. I know lockers had fallen through to the floor below and wellington boots, which had been in the lockers, had melted. We had no windows in the telephone exchange [Hertford Street] and very few lines working, but we sat there most of the day.[86]

We were alive: now for the walk home to find our families. The crater stretching from one side of Binley Road to the other was very deep. A young woman, an air raid warden, was swinging a lantern to warn approaching rescue vehicles of one more hazard in their way. The road was littered with more bits of jagged metal from spent shells than I had ever seen before that night. I hurried on, confident that all was well at home.

It was. Apart from an unexploded incendiary bomb which had penetrated the ground floor window of our neighbour's house, our homes were safe. When I unlocked the door, Mother was already boiling a kettle of water on an electric fire turned on its side. There was no gas, but we had mains electric power and water, unlike many parts of the city, which had none. When we listened to the news broadcast there was confirmation, if needed, that the city was out of action. The world was informed that Coventry had been the target of an air raid as heavy as any inflicted on London. We did not disagree.

My job was to get to Hertford Street, to my office, without delay. What I would find, how we would get the paper [the *Midland Daily Telegraph*] out, I did not know. But, as I rode over my usual route, dismounted to avoid street rubble, I was appalled at what confronted me. There was no straight run to the centre of town. Detours were necessary as fires were burning, timbers toppling, and new craters barred the way. I pushed my bike into battered Broadgate and found myself momentarily disorientated. In the smoke-laden atmosphere, with the smell of burning all around, mounds of rubble remained of lines of once-attractive shop fronts. Whole streets had gone and, although the proud spire of St Michael's Cathedral still pushed its tip towards the gloomy sky, there was nothing behind the tower. The nave, chancel, side chapels, all were roofless, a mass of debris; the blasphemy of the night was revealed — factories, offices, shops, houses, even hospitals and churches might suffer, but we should not lose our Cathedral.

On the great west window of the neighbouring church of the Holy Trinity, where Mum and Dad had married in 1919, was the message of encouragement in large letters for all to see, as on every wartime morning:

"IT ALL DEPENDS ON ME AND I DEPEND ON GOD"

My way to Hertford Street that frightful Friday was among the thin lines of people picking their way, straggling in all directions, shocked into silence. We had purpose, but at quarter speed, and it seemed futile. There was no work to go to in the city centre: nothing to do immediately except to try to absorb the enormity of the unreal scenes around us. But the nightmare was only too real. The facade of the *Telegraph* building still stood, but little remained of the plant behind the front offices...... Except for a tangled mass of twisted machinery throughout the plant, there was nothing to convey that, only a day earlier, the whole building had been charged with life and purpose. The ruined presses were dead. Their loss was almost personal.[98]

Looking from Broadgate, past Owen Owen, down towards the old market,
with Corporation Street in the distance

The principal shopping and office centre, consisting of both old and new buildings, was not only gutted, but was a mass of ruin and devastation. An earthquake could not have rendered the scene more desolate or distressing.

Almost every factory, if not actually hit, could not function through an entire disorganisation of the utility services of water, gas, electricity and transport.

The control of the situation for the time being became completely out of hand; the telephone service, except for one line, was rendered useless, and there was no other means of communication available.[31]

In the ghostly quiet of the morning, I started walking with my parents to the city centre. They were worried about my grandparents.

I knew things must be bad in the centre because I had left the shelter once during the night to go into the house and watch from my bedroom. But all I could see were the three spires above the flames.

On our walk through the uncanny silence we hardly met a soul. It was as though everyone was dead. Many people were, but most had survived and were still in a state of shock.

We reached the top of Bishop Street. A big crater was where Nan's shop had been standing. She was all right, though.

The maternity wing of the Coventry and Warwickshire Hospital was wrecked. We ploughed on through the debris to see if my grandparents had come through. Going through Broadgate was terrible, but when we came to the Cathedral, it was still burning. The pigeons that had fallen from the spire were still burning on the floor. It was an awful sight. As we gazed at the still burning altar, a policeman fetched us away.

When we got to High Street, we couldn't get across because it was blocked by a pile of wreckage from houses and shops. It was as high as the Council House clock nearby. Anyhow, we scrambled to the top and came down the other side after getting all filthy. But we weren't worried — we were alive.[64]

Tragic spectre of the Cathedral

By early morning the Cathedral presented the same appearance of tragic yet dignified desolation which all notice who have seen it since. Every roof is gone and the whole Cathedral lies open to the sky. The matchless pillars, arcades and clerestories of the nave, chancel and aisles are lying on the ground in long piles of broken masonry where they fell.

The encircling outer walls of the chapels and the sanctuary stand in an unbroken line, completely enclosing the ruins within the sacred ground. The walls of the five-sided apse are standing with the traceries slightly damaged. The south porch, which was part of the older church existing before the tower and spire or any part of St Michael's was built, is standing safely, owing probably to its groined roof.

The tower and spire are blackened on the side, where the volumes of smoke engulfed them for a while, but otherwise they are as strong as ever.

All those who have passionately loved this most beautiful building, as thousands of Coventry citizens have done, feel a grief which cannot possibly be expressed in words.[32]

Journeys across devastation

The next morning my Mum and I set out to return the children to their home at Cheylesmore, on the other side of the city. The devastation was horrifying. So many familiar landmarks gone, as we walked down Bishop Street from Radford Road and on through Broadgate.

There were burning buildings on all sides, folks digging in the ruins. I remember a bus burning in Broadgate and seeing our beloved Cathedral a burning ruin, but its spire unbelievably still standing in defiance.

As we went down Little Park Street, I was shocked to see that Bushills had become one of the smoking ruins. We had difficulty getting through to Cheylesmore as there were unexploded bombs which caused diversions. I do know we went round the back of London Road cemetery. I remember this especially as, when we attempted to return that way after having delivered the children to my sister's house, we were stopped by an air raid warden and told we couldn't go that way because there was an unexploded bomb just over the cemetery wall. So close we lived to death in those days.[77]

As with difficulty they approached the centre of the city an uncanny and fearful sight met their gaze. Although the Cathedral's spire was standing erect, the centre of Coventry was devastated and to reach the spot where Bushill's factory had once stood, they had to pick their way over piles of rubble and masonry and pass by smouldering fires and twisted girders. When at last they arrived at Cow Lane, Bushills was still burning fiercely......

There was no running water nor, indeed, any other means of combatting the flames, and all that he [Ernie King of Bushills] and his colleagues could do was stand at a safe distance, for the heat was intense, and watch helplessly.[69]

Daylight the following morning was a nightmare!...... I was single and lived in the Stoke area of Coventry in those days with my parents. The roads were strewn with craters and rubble and it was almost impossible to ride a cycle for any great distance.

I started home via Station Street West, Station Street East, onto the Stoney Stanton Road, and more or less had to carry my bike on my shoulder most of the way. When I got as far as Red Lane, the AFS [Auxiliary Fire Service] was playing its hoses on what was left of the cinema......I remember asking one of the firemen, who had his back to me, whether it was possible to get through Red Lane to the Stoke Heath area. When he turned round, it proved to be Billy Morgan, the pre-war Coventry City goalkeeper, and he was as black as the ace of spades!

I can remember being told that it was possible to get through Red Lane, but he warned me that one bomb had just missed the big bag of the old Ordnance Depot and had dropped in the road, making a large crater. Large crater it was, all right. I walked up the embankment it had created with my bike on my shoulder and, when I looked down from the summit, it looked like a minor Vesuvius!

Crossing the canal, I made it to Stoke Heath and Mercer Avenue. A land mine, complete with parachute, had caught on the branches of one of the trees bordering Mercer Avenue and was swinging to and fro, clear of terra firma, in a gentle breeze.

Arriving home, I found a land mine had dropped in Burlington Road and the blast from this explosion had blown all the slates off the roof of our own house and torn out all the window frames. The most remarkable feature, apart from the fact that the house was untenable, was the fact that our canary was singing in its cage like a chief stoker and the budgerigar was also still alive and well, so obviously the blast from the land mine must have sucked the windows and doors outwards.

Naturally, we had to remove all the furniture and contents of our home and store them until other suitable accommodation could be found.[39]

It took railway lorry driver Reg Hughes a whole working day to cross Coventry on an urgent delivery. With a desperately needed set of railway points on his wagon, he had to pick his way through rubble-filled streets, constantly being turned back by unexploded bombs and impassable roads......

The crump of delayed action bombs going off followed him on his slow crawl through a nightmare landscape. In a street close to the city centre, he saw rescue workers pulling bodies from a smashed house. At the goods yard a river of molten sugar was all that remained of a food store that had taken a direct hit. And a pall of smoke hung over the city centre from a still-burning meat warehouse in Little Park Street.

For a man whose job had already given him an encyclopaedic knowledge of the city's layout, the destruction wrought by a single night of air raids came as a considerable shock.[71]

Make a cup of tea

After the All Clear went, Mum decided to make a pot of tea. I still do not know why she was emptying the teapot outside but, as one of our neighbours was coming round the corner into the back yard, he got all the tea leaves over him. The poor chap had just come home from the pit. Along with all the other miners, he had been stuck at the bottom of the shaft. In order not to show any lights, they could not bring the 2 pm–10 pm shift up, so they had been forced to stay down there an extra nine hours.

He was very cold and to have cold tea over him just finished his day for him. But, after letting his family know he was all right, they all came in our house for a fresh cup of tea. The house was warm as Mum had kept the fire on all night (it was an old fashioned range). Then, on the Sunday, my Auntie, Uncle and their three sons turned up on our doorstep, just with what they stood up in. They had had a direct hit by a land mine on their house and they had been wandering round just anywhere for three days. So, only naturally, we made room for them......

[On the nineteenth] my Auntie took me with her into the city centre, from where we had to walk to Coundon, where she lived. It was terrible passing one funeral place. All the bodies covered up were outside and people were still wandering round and crying. Now it seems like a bad dream.[62]

Claiming for new clothes

My Dad walked to Bell Green and we went to Holyhead Road. Our place hadn't any roof on and was a proper mess. No work could be done and the owner's son offered the men 2/6[d] an hour to clear the factory up. Some did, but the girls signed on at the labour exchange. 10/- a week we had, but we were only on it for about three days and then back to work.

Dad and Tom boarded the front door up and we managed the best we could. We were told to go to a place opposite the Council House to claim for what we had lost. They had got clothes that had been sent to them from all round the country to give bombed out folk. We didn't have anything, but lots of people did; suits, underclothes, dresses and even overcoats and fur coats. One girl we knew had a fur coat given, and she thought she was the cat's miaow. We were given ten pounds for me and Tom and ten pounds for Mum and Dad.[60]

Foraging for food

The first thing we had to think about was **food**. My sisters and I went foraging: the butcher had a big notice up, "Bombed out, but not gone out". One of us queued for sausages, which we fried over the open fire as we had no gas. One queued for bread at a baker's where each customer was sold half a loaf. We had no water but over the weeks we queued for water at the water vehicle which came round or we boiled the rainwater from the tank. We took lemonade bottles to work and queued for water as the firm had its own water tank……

People who had been bombed out queued for a clothes voucher at St Mary's Hall, then went along to the Drapers Hall for their clothes. Big tables lined the hall full of clothes, some from overseas, others given locally. I worked there, helping to fit out the people as they filed past…… I received a little old granny and her five year old granddaughter. They had spent the night in the shelter and were safe. The rest of the family had been killed in a direct hit on the house.

A WVS officer put her hand on my shoulder and whispered to me, "Give her all you've got," which I proceeded to do. As well as underwear, shoes, top clothes for both, I gave them soap, flannels, towels, toothbrush and tooth paste, and a blanket each.

Lastly, a woollen hood for the little one and a warm scarf for Granny, plus a kiss for the child.[7]

First meal

We were in a state of shock, suffering from torn off finger-nails, cuts and bruises. I had a broken big toe and nose, and my sister a broken arm, as had one of my friends, done in a desperate bid to dig ourselves free from the rubble. We were hungry, tired and cold. Neither help nor advice was at hand. So, passing a shop on Stoney Stanton Road, where we had wandered looking for help, I saw bread and tinned soup in the window, through a badly cracked pane. There was no reply to our knocking and shouting, so I took a brick and pushed the window in, helping myself to a loaf of bread and three cans of soup. I punched holes in the tins, we pulled the bread to pieces as best we could manage, very difficult with blood on our hands and faces, and damaged finger nails. But our teeth were good and we managed. It was beautiful bread, soup, and 'blood'! Then at last we found help, but not before we were sick, throwing up that lovely soup and bread.

The wardens on duty took us to a van and gave us warm tea, then on to a first aid post, where we were crudely patched up. It was no use going to the hospital, as it was in a terrible state. But a doctor did set our broken bones. We were given a ticket for a train journey home, or anywhere, to get us out of the city. So, just as we stood up, in dirty work overalls, absolutely filthy from head to foot, we walked to Bedworth where we found transport to take us to join the evacuation train to the North.[81]

Mobile food canteens

I can recall the mobile food canteens on Pool Meadow and can actually remember the late Alderman and Councillor Pearl Hyde, as a member of the WVS, distributing food to the bombed out, and remember a delayed action bomb exploding in the old Triumph works in Dale Street, off Cope Street, on which part of the Polytechnic now stands. Firemen and rescue people were virtually throwing us underneath the mobile canteen vehicles and I clearly remember debris, showering down on the roofs of these vehicles. [20]

Rest centres used by homeless

St Thomas's Rest Centre comprised two rooms, a general room and a dormitory. The general room was about twenty-four feet in width and forty feet in length. There was a good fire and round it four easy chairs and a sofa. Half a dozen hard chairs were scattered about the room. There were three women and a man, all middle-aged, and two children in the room, sitting round the fire drinking tea served by the vicar. In the dormitory there were a dozen beds. The vicar took us to the kitchen to see the supplies: bread sent by the Ministry of Health, butter and bully beef. Water for tea was boiled on the fire in the general room.[92]

This and the handful of other rest centres not destroyed had to cope with thousands of homeless. In the horrendous circumstances, unforeseen by anyone, and despite the great work they did, they proved totally inadequate. Above all, they were not able to provide long-term shelter, nor deal with the pyschological impact the devastation caused.

Just before dawn the All Clear sounded and, later, the dispatch riders began to arrive back at Grove House, some with buckled wheels, punctured tyres, bent footrests, twisted handlebars, and torn battledress but, miraculously, no one was seriously injured, only cuts and bruises. As they stood around, discussing the night's events, a police car arrived and the driver, an Inspector, hatless and dirt-stained, said, "Colonel Pugh wants you all to go to the temporary mortuaries and help to keep the people out".

Six riders went to the Hill Street gasworks, where a horrific scene met their eyes. Hundreds of corpses lay around, piled haphazardly, some minus limbs, others partially burnt. Of particular harrowing impact was the body of a little girl clutching a rag doll, sightless eyes staring at the smoke laden sky.

Crowds of distraught people were moving among the bodies, pushing some aside to see who was underneath, searching for loved ones or relatives. A Home Guard Captain approached the dispatch riders, saying, "For Christ's sake, get these people out of here. Use force if you have to, but get them out!"

The six dispatch riders commenced shepherding the citizens out of the yard. Most were shocked and went without protest, but one or two women struggled fiercely, screaming and shouting, and had to be carried out.

When order was restored and the gates locked, the Home Guard Captain asked the dispatch riders if they had eaten. When told they had had their last meal the previous day, he said, "You'll have to stay here until you are relieved, but there are some WVS mobile canteens about, so I'll ask them to call".

Towards noon, a mobile canteen drove into the yard, stopping short of the nearest bodies, and commenced to dispense mugs of tea and sandwiches. The brave WVS ladies served the food and drink with apparent unconcern, despite the macabre surroundings. The overpowering stench of burnt human flesh is not conducive to eating but, as the danger was past, hunger asserted itself and the dispatch riders consumed the food voraciously.

At mid-afternoon a detachment of the Army Medical Corps arrived and the dispatch riders were grateful to get home and to bed, thankful they were not among the thousands of casualties of that evil night.[103]

Apart from the Army Medical Corps, Herbert Morrison, the Home Secretary, drafted in the Pioneer Corps and soon a thousand [some say eighteen

hundred] troops and twelve hundred building workers, especially released from the Army, were helping to repair the devastation.

I worked in the offices of a bakery in Maudsley Road and, after spending nearly every night in our Anderson shelter, we often had to walk to work the next morning in the middle of the road while buildings were still burning on both sides and everywhere looked like a battlefield......

My boyfriend, who later became my husband, was stationed at Budbrooke Barracks and was called into Coventry, first to direct the traffic and later on to dig up bodies that were buried beneath the rubble.[14]

Mrs Watson had left her parents in Coventry to join many spending the night in Leamington Spa. The next day she began the task of trying to find them again:

We heard the next morning that Coventry was on fire and I and a bus load of other people were only allowed as far as Kenilworth. We were told we wouldn't be allowed into Coventry, but we were detemined and walked all around Crackley Woods. I must have passed dozens of unexploded bombs.

My husband's factory [which was Nuffield Mechanisations, on Gosford Street and made Bofors guns] was on fire and, as we walked down Gulson Road, all buses and coaches were parked outside the hospital, all being used as ambulances. Little did I know that my Dad was in one, as when I heard the terrible news that my Mother and Auntie had been killed outright, we were told he had been taken to hospital, but which one was not known. So my husband and I travelled to Rugby, Warwick and various other hospitals looking for him, and we eventually found out he had died on the nineteenth, in Gulson Hospital.[126]

We visited my eldest brother, who was looking after his ten day old baby girl. His wife had had to go to hospital, which was heavily bombarded and she had been evacuated. Where to, he didn't know and it took him a few days to locate her. So while that went on, Mother and I packed baby's requirements and took her to our relations in the country. What a journey *that* was. Five vehicles to cover forty miles. When we walked into my Auntie and Uncle's, they broke down, thinking we had all perished after seeing the fire glows and noise in the sky.[61]

Not only did her relations see the glow, forty miles away, but witnesses as far apart as Wolverhampton and Gloucester also saw the ominous halo over the burning city.

141

Bomb Disposal Squads

They dropped a delayed action bomb on the cottages in Bulls Head Lane and they fetched the Bomb Disposal Squad in to remove it. They found it had gone into the cottages and under the road. Those soldiers were marvellous with the folks of the district, for many were scared, but they put their minds at ease. After they had removed the bomb, all those folks had a whip round for them and they returned to the New Sun for a quick one.[60]

The bravery of the Bomb Disposal Squad saved the row of houses from being completely flattened. We were told afterwards that, if the bomb had gone off on impact, many lives would have been lost, even though we were in an Anderson shelter at the bottom of the garden. The row of houses would have disappeared.

I remember when the Disposal Squad boarded their open lorry outside the Red Lane School gates to depart, all the residents of that area lustily cheered and clapped them and threw gifts of cigarettes, flowers and money onto the lorry. It was with a lump of pride in my throat that I threw my small token of gratitude.

The courage and bravery of those young men was beyond words or description. They were the unsung heroes of the Second World War.[115]

Reg was driving his lorry down London Road, on his way to Whitley Aerodrome when he spotted three schoolboys watching bomb disposal men at work on a massive unexploded bomb.

He stopped and shouted at them for being too close to the team, who were straddling the device and working on it with stethoscopes.

As he turned away it went off, blowing him over and leaving him stone deaf for two days. The schoolboys had moved out of range just in time, but the bomb disposal team, all bar one, were in pieces.[71]

Another horrible memory was the fate of a Bomb Disposal Squad who removed a delayed action bomb from premises in Swanswell Street. My route [as a bus driver] took me down Daventry Road behind the soldiers' vehicle. On Whitley Common, frequently used for detonating bombs and as a dumping ground for bomb damage rubble, I saw the men start to slide the bomb to the ground.

The next thing — woof! A big flash of orange and I saw a man running across the common without a stitch on. The soldier escaped unhurt, but all his comrades were killed.[55]

School roll of death

There was no school that day. Mayor-making used to be in November and the new Mayor always gave schools a Friday holiday. 15 November was our Mayor's holiday.

Windows blown in, ceilings down, slates off the roof, no gas, no water, and no electricity. I remember sweeping up my gold watch with my bedroom plaster.

Following previous instructions, we had to report bomb damage at once. We went into town to report. Broadgate was flattened and the Cathedral burnt out. The heart had gone out of Coventry.

On Monday there came the problem of how to get to school. Buses could not get along their normal routes owing to bomb craters and the tram lines were cut in many places. On Stoney Stanton Road we could get as far as Broad Street, then, as there were two separate bomb damages, we had quite a long walk before reaching another tram to take us to Bell Green. Later, buses were introduced on this service.[8]

18th: School assembled — nine present and two members of staff. Miss R— and Miss A— were both casualties. Miss R— soon arrived, Miss A— could not be traced. She was traced several days later. No hot dinners were obtainable and there was no transport. Only eleven children appeared at all during the week.

Teachers and girls again visited and tried to trace the children; it was found that four girls had died:

Florence B—	31.1.29
Ada B—	26.3.30
Daisy T—	4.12.28
Muriel S—	25.2.30

R.I.P.[28]

The hunt must go on!

At four o'clock on the morning of 15 November, Assistant Divisional Fire Officer Geoffrey Blackstone was awoken from his bed and requested to get to Coventry as quickly as possible:

"There's been a heavy raid on Coventry. Get over there. They want two hundred London firemen."

One hour later, after a hasty breakfast, I set off at top speed. In a village some miles from the city centre, I stopped short. A huntsman in a pink coat and black cap hat loomed like a ghost rider from the early morning mist, peremptorily calling upon me to halt. As I watched incredulously, a pack of thirty foxhounds rumbled slowly across the road and vanished from sight. With mingled anger and disbelief, I thought, 'Coventry may burn to the ground, but England's still going on.' [21]

As he entered the city, he found it gutted completely. 43,000 of the city's 75,000 houses had been damaged in some way and twenty-seven war production factories had been hit. For many, still cowering in their Anderson shelters, the only notice they had that the raid was over was the wardens coming round and shouting, "It's all over". For many people, it felt as though their lives were as well.

The city centre lay in ruins, grotesque, twisted, smouldering, the streets plastered in red mud and debris. Silent, staring groups gathered before landmarks or shops, perhaps waiting for the owners to return. The Government Meat Store exuded the acrid smell of roasted carcasses. The war correspondent of the *Daily Express*, Hilda Marchant, wrote, as she watched the exodus of thousands of silent, fleeing refugees pushing prams and barrows stacked high with the pathetic remains of personal belongings out into the countryside:

It was a familiar sight, one I had seen in Spain and Finland. Yet this was worse...... These people moved against a background of suburban villas, had English faces, used the English tongue, wore English clothes. They were our own kind......[89]

Most stayed, though. Even if it meant sitting amongst the rubble, boiling a battered kettle on a fire made of wood from their rafters, searching for lost possessions amongst bricks, shattered wardrobes and smashed cupboards, huddled in a torn blanket or dusty best coat in a roofless kitchen, or waving at the neighbours as they dusted the ledge below a glassless window, they stayed, determined to clean up the mess and get back to as normal a life as possible.

Shops and banks defiantly opened. The staff of Barclays stood on bricks to avoid the pools of water around them, with no heating or light, and with all the windows blown out. Before they opened, they had to dig through the rubble to get to their strongrooms.

Marks and Spencer opened proudly, proclaiming, "Messrs Marks and Spencer of Smithford Street are playing their part in defying the activities of the Hun by opening up in Whitefriars Street". That day too, the papers were back on the streets, sometimes inaccurate, occasionally hiding or distorting the depressed mood of the city and the effectiveness of the city's resistance, but describing the full horror of the previous night to both Coventrians and the world.

Midland Daily Telegraph
Friday 15 November 1940

Coventry bombed: casualties 1,000
Cathedral and shelters hit

"The city of Coventry was heavily attacked last night," states a Ministry of Home Security communiqué issued this afternoon. "The scale of the raids was comparable with those of the largest night attacks on London.

"The enemy were heavily engaged by intensive AA fire which kept them at a great height and hindered accurate bombing of industrial targets, but the city itself suffered very seriously.

"Preliminary reports indicate that the number of casualties may be in the neighbourhood of a thousand."

The headline above this article boldly stated that, "Berlin gets biggest bombing ever". It seems only tens of planes were involved, not hundreds. Also, most witnesses testify that the anti-aircraft guns were not effective and, once they had run out of ammunition, the Germans were left free to bomb the city indiscriminately and at whatever height they chose.

Waves of enemy planes in dusk to dawn raid

......At least 40 enemy planes came over in waves from dusk till dawn. Casualties included members of the Civil Defence, fire and polices services, known to have lost their lives while engaged on duty.

Among the places damaged was the operating theatre of a hospital, but the hospital is now working as a clearing station."

Feeding centres
An isolation hospital was hit and, in one ward, some casualties were caused.

"Two churches, public baths, two clubs, a school, an hotel, four public shelters, cinemas, a police station, a post office, and two first aid posts were damaged.

Steps are being taken to shepherd the homeless to the feeding centres which have been prepared.[94]

Not only is the figure for German planes missing a nought, but four churches and four schools were hit, many city centre hotels were devastated, four first aid posts were damaged and six out of the twelve [or thirteen] rest centres knocked out, making the last sentence highly dubious. Although these centres had cared for some three thousand people between August and November, after the 14/15 November raid, the six remaining were full to

overflowing, and proved totally inadequate. However, the rest centres were well stocked with food. There, the homeless received hot drinks, breakfasts, cleaning facilities, hot midday and evening meals and plenty of tea.

Daily Herald
Saturday 16 November 1940

Nazis say 30,000 fire bombs fell

......Berlin radio claimed that five hundred planes took part in the raid and that five hundred tons of high explosive and thirty thousand incendiary bombs were dropped.

"These," said the German High Command, "caused tremendous devastation" and fires that were visible from the Channel coast a hundred and twenty-five miles away.

The raid was described by Berlin as a reprisal for the RAF attack on Munich, and was held to be the greatest bombardment in the history of warfare.

Apparently, the Luftwaffe was striving to make Coventry a second Guernica.

At times the attack took the form of dive bombing and machinegunning.

"The people of Coventry," the Ministry of Home Security stated, "bore their ordeal with great courage."

"......bore their ordeal with great courage"! This was the "official line". "Coventry tackles great problem confidently," proclaimed the *Midland Daily Telegraph* on the eighteenth, with the city, "well launched on the way to reconstruction". The next day it was, "Coventry's 'carry-on' spirit", whilst, "Civilians, however, went about their allotted tasks with a spirit of determination that has aroused the admiration of Britain." Such empty boasting only served to undermine the morale of Coventrians even further. They could see the total devastation around them and were desperate not to provoke any further raids. Protests flooded into the Emergency Committee, begging for such bravado to stop.

The same issue of the *Daily Herald* carried the following article on its front page:

Coventry homeless slept by roadside this morning
Midlands city is now like a bombarded French town
Not a mortal blow: work will restart

Coventry has been the victim of the most concentrated, if not the worst, raid since the war began. I have just come back from the centre of the city, which now looks exactly like one of those French towns that were laid level during the last war by an intensive bombardment. The Cathedral is in ruins except for its tower and, over a large area surrounding it, there lies the stench of burning houses.

The number of casualties cannot yet be determined, but it is certainly large. (Preliminary reports, says the Ministry of Home Security, indicate that the number of casualties may number a thousand.) The damage which has been inflicted on this city must run into millions of pounds.

I was told by one of the inhabitants that the noise of falling bombs was practically continuous and that, after a short time, everyone was literally dazed by the noise.

I approached the city from Rugby and, a few miles out of the city, I encountered the first large body of refugees walking along the roadside, exactly as the Belgians and French escaped from the last German invasion.

Children were being carried in their fathers' arms and pushed along in perambulators. Luggage was piled high in perambulators.

There were suitcases and bundles on people's shoulders; little families trudged along hand in hand with rugs, blankets and, in fact, anything they could have salvaged from their ruined homes. There were also many motor cars parked by the roadside in which people would pass the night, despite the intense cold.

Under the hedgerows
Nevertheless, those with motor cars will be luckier than those without. For, despite the hospitality of surrounding towns and villages, it will have been impossible for everyone to get a bed, or even shelter. I saw several people making preparations to lie down under the leeside of buildings, or against hedgerows......

On my way to the Cathedral I encountered a girl of, perhaps, twelve years of age and I asked her what she was doing. The air was thick with smoke and a fire was still blazing in a house not twenty yards away.

"Oh," she said, "I'm just looking around." I asked her where she was going to sleep that night and she replied, "Why, here of course. We were lucky."

"Have you any water or gas?" I asked.

"No," she said, "but we'll do some cooking on an oil stove and the water will turn up from somewhere."[41]

Ernie Pile, of the *Boston Sunday Globe,* visited the city some months later. His account of the devastation still around and of what eye witnesses told him is very powerful. This is the report he sent back to America:

You can drive out of Coventry today in any direction and on the outskirts of the town you'll see vast fields solidly covered with dumped truckloads of brickbats and rubble. As a Coventry friend of mine said, "There are probably more secondhand bricks here today than anywhere else in the world".

While downtown wreckage is being cleared up and hauled away, most of Coventry's ruins still have to lie where they are until this little misunderstanding with Germany has been cleared up. Coventry will not look like a normal city again until many years after the war.

Coventry is carrying on as best it can. Everybody is back at work, but few people live normally. A good portion of the population is living in single rooms salvaged from shattered homes. There is plenty of food in the shops now, but the shops are so few that there is always a long line of people waiting on the sidewalk to get in.

Once more the beautiful girls of Coventry (and I mean *really* beautiful) grace the streets. And, best of all, the dog races have started again. The profits go to the relief of Coventry's bomb victims.

Coventry represents to Americans, and to most Englishmen too, the all-out, one-night blitz at its worst...... I have seen so much hideous carnage in London that you could no longer call me an amateur at viewing wreckage. Yet, in spite of all that, when we drove into Coventry today my emotions were those of profound shock. I was horrified.

We walked and drove around for three hours. And, late in the afternoon, I realised that I had been saying to myself out loud, over and over again like a chant, "My God, this is awful!"

The centre of Coventry is in ruins. Many of the hotels are gone. A big newspaper office is a jumble of wilted presses and linotype machines. You can stand on what used to be a main corner in downtown Coventry and, in three directions, see nothing but waste. You can walk down what was once a street in ankle-deep mud. On each side, tractors and cranes and men with blow torches are untangling and hauling away twisted girders and mangled rubble.

Nobody has ever been able to put that night of Coventry's into words. The noise was fiendish. It seemed that the entire city was burning down. The only reason a large part of the population didn't lie dead the next morning is that they took to the shelters. They say the final death toll was just a little over five hundred. It seems almost impossible that the loss of life should have been no more than that. For Coventry is a city of a quarter of a million people.

The city had two mass burials, with more than two hundred bodies in each. And such is Coventry's opinion of the Germans that they kept the time of the funerals secret, for fear of a blitz directed at the mourners. Scores of bodies were unidentified. The only way the death of some of the people was known was from the fact that their families never saw them again. I feel certain that they will still be finding bodies in Coventry long after the war is over.

We walked through a street that was a no-man's land. Utter destruction lay on both sides. One side had been brick houses, the other side a warehouse. Now both sides were just piles of broken brick. We turned into an alley that had been cleared. A jumble of bricks had been pushed back from the line of the alley and a little picket fence built around them. Back in the alley, we found

J B Shelton. He is living in a lean-to about the size of a double bed. J B hunted around for a couple of boards and laid them across boxes for us to sit on. The debris we had passed used to be J B Shelton's house and office. In fact, he had owned four houses in a row. They all make one big heap now......

"Where were you on the night of the blitz?" I asked him.

"Where was I?" he said. "I was right here, right here in this alley, running up and down all night long. My house was already afire, so I just tried to save the stables," he said. His five horses were tied in their stalls in a frame building running along the alley at the back of the house. "All night I was running up and down the side of these stables, like this, throwing water on the boards. I got the water out of that open tank there.

"Around midnight I got the horses all out. They took it fine. I had two sacks ready to put over their heads, but I only had to do that on one of them. I took them out two at a time, so they wouldn't be scared...... All night long the planes were diving right down on top of us. Say, I'll never see anything like it again in my lifetime. I wouldn't have missed it for anything in the world!"[101]

So many were now without homes and suffering the loss of members of their families. Roads out of the city were thronged with people making their way on foot with what belongings they could carry, in search of a temporary roof.

We had relatives in Leamington who sought us out and begged us to join them, if only for a few weeks' rest. It took four days to make up our minds. Eventually, when my parents and sister, who were living with us after being bombed out, were all out for various reasons, I agreed that, for our baby's sake, we should go. We packed a few things and, with the baby's gas helmet anchored under the pram, we set off to walk to Leamington, transport being practically non-existent.

As we left our home behind I wondered if we should ever see it again. It took us three hours to reach The Parade [in Leamington] and, as we dragged wearily along, we could hear people saying, "Look, some more refugees from Coventry".[10]

Mass Observation sent three observers to monitor the mood of Coventrians immediately after the blitz. Their report makes stark reading and belies the official and newspaper stories about solid resolve and redoubled morale. It states that everywhere there was despondency. "Coventry is finished...... Coventry is dead" were common complaints. "People feel the town itself is dead, finished, the only thing to do is to get out altogether." Because of its small size and the intense devastation, many people flocked out, never to return. "The small size of the place makes people feel that the only thing they can do is to get out of it altogether."

It continues: "There were more open signs of hysteria, terror, neurosis observed in one evening than during the whole of the past two months together in all areas. Women were seen to cry, to scream, to tremble all over, to faint in the street, to attack a fireman, and so on...... There were several signs of suppressed panic as darkness approached. In two cases, people were seen fighting to get onto cars which they thought would take them out into the country, though, in fact, the drivers insisted the cars were going just up the road to a garage."

During the raid, it states how people had been "staggering about with shock, as though they were hopelessly drunk". It concludes that far more should have been done to treat the psychological consequences of the terror bombing, to care for people's mental state and deal with their shock and bereavement. Whilst fire brigades, police forces and army detachments were quickly brought in, no extra social service help was available. "The whole tempo could have been altered if the authorities had spent five per cent of their effort on the survivors, eg, on mobile canteens, loudspeaker vans to give information, newspapers delivered to the streets, social workers."[92]

Incongruously, Ritchie Calder, in a report on Air Raid Morale for the Foreign Office in 1941 stated that the Coventry raids had not resulted in a single case of neurosis. I'm sure the Foreign Office rested assured.

A Chiefs of Staff paper commented that:

The morale of the workers in Coventry has unquestionably deteriorated as a result of air attacks. War production has attracted a large population from other parts of the country. These people naturally are not imbued with the same civic patriotism, and consequently do not have the same anchors as the long-established inhabitants of other provincial towns or London. Coventry, moreover, is a small town and the effect of bombing is therefore more concentrated than in the case of large towns.

On the other hand, many people were full of resolution. They gritted their teeth and refused to get downhearted. Many felt that, if they could stick it out, they'd beat the Germans in the end. Recovery, when it started, went ahead quickly and efficiently. Factories rapidly began producing again, even with roofs off and piles of debris around. This report on the activities of the Home Guard shows this well:

Friday 15 November: I arranged for a number of guards, with reliefs, to be posted at danger areas during the day and, in addition, collected a number of men to act as rescue parties, work being carried out chiefly in the Spon Street area where, apart from rescue work, men were engaged in clearing a passage through the streets and assisting in traffic control. They were engaged for the

A postman searches for an address amidst the ruins of Smithford Street

whole day till dusk and I must add that, despite food difficulties, they worked really well.

Saturday 16 November: Further working parties were arranged for this day and street clearing, traffic control, etc, was carried out, whilst one party of about sixteen men were engaged in digging out bodies from the rear of the [–] Club, where twelve people had been killed. This party was engaged at this spot for the whole of the day, working under great difficulty and with a DA [Delayed Action bomb] eight yards away. Men were also in Earlsdon. Further guards were posted at the bottom of Hearsall Lane and Kingsland Avenue for, in the the area between these points, nineteen DAs had been located.

Towards the end of the afternoon, several men assisted the police at

Hearsall Common, both with traffic control and with the business of getting people transported outside the city area. Hundreds of people were congregated at this point, and as the police were from Birmingham and therefore strangers to the place, the difficulties will be apparent.

Having heard that the Home Guard at the Gauge and Tool Company had so far taken no part in anything, I visited the factory and interviewed Captain [–], the Officer Commanding. I found that from twelve noon the factory was closed till Monday. On asking what had been or was being done, I was told that they "were waiting for instructions from the police," and had therefore done nothing so far. I am afraid that I was rather pointed in my remarks, but the outcome was that a parade was called at twelve o'clock and I believe that Captain [–] got parties of men working in the Earlsdon district on the Saturday afternoon and the Sunday.

I also got in touch with Standard Aero and they sent a few men down to the Spon Street district and Earlsdon, together with several armoured cars, which we used for transporting people outside the city.

Sunday 17 November: Again, a party was working at the [-] Club and further parties were engaged in salvage work, street cleaning and traffic control, in addition to the barrier guards in danger areas. This was carried out during the whole of the day. At the [–] Club, eight bodies had been recovered by the evening.

Monday 18 November: The working party resumed at the [–] Club and a programme similar to that of the day before was carried out. By the afternoon, the remaining bodies had been recovered. This was a gruesome task, especially to the younger element, since it was a case of collecting odd limbs and fragments and the smell was very bad. However, the men stuck to it well and the job was accomplished. All this time work had been carried on within a few yards of a DA, which fortunately had not exploded during operations, and which was removed in the early afternoon. By now, most of the DAs in the Allesley Old Road area had either exploded or had been removed and I withdrew the guards from this area.

Tuesday 19 November: One man of this Company happened to state that the firm for which he worked, Harvey and Son, wholesale general dealers, had had a large warehouse at Priestley's Bridge destroyed and that there was a very large amount of stock, mostly foodstuffs, to be salvaged. I arranged accordingly that a party of men should proceed there to give what assistance was possible.

This party worked at this place each day throughout the week until Saturday 23 November, commencing at 9 am and finishing at dusk......At the moment the personnel of the Company appears to be very scattered, with bombing out of homes and evacuations. It is impossible at present to contact many of these as I have received no notification of their whereabouts.

At Cash's Kingsfield Road factory, repair work started almost immediately:

The spectacle at daylight was indeed terrible, with fires still burning in many places, a thick pall of smoke over everything and roads mostly impassable owing to fallen debris, bomb craters and unexploded bombs.

This was our first experience of a heavy air bombardment and the appearance of Kingfield was such as to make one think that it would be a long time indeed before anything could be done again. We were also without electricity, gas or water for the best part of a week.

The actual loss of machinery in the attack was not considerable, amounting to about a dozen looms in the Long Shop, but the loss of so much glass and the damaged roofs exposed much of our machinery to the winter weather; our machinery, moreover, is such that even a comparatively short exposure to rain and damp results in serious damage.

The one bright spot in the days which followed was the wonderful spirit shown by so many of our employees, many of whom had lost their own homes. There was no lack of volunteers to help with the first aid repairs; even on the morning after the attack women and girls were sweeping up debris and trying to restore some sort of order in their departments. Felt was nailed up where the glass had gone and tarpaulins were fixed over the more extensive gaps......

Makeshift repairs proceeded apace; electricity, gas and water were gradually restored and, after some few days, smoke once more appeared from the Kingfield chimney stack, a most cheering sight......[6]

Throughout the city, the dedication of the workforce was the same. Recognising that they were frontline troops, they cleared debris away, repaired machines and worked twelve hour shifts, seven days a week in factories exposed to the elements, among buckled girders and crumbled walls, without light or heating, showing remarkable dedication. Immediately after the raid twelve thousand of them were unemployed, but within two weeks nearly ten thousand were back at work. The Alvis was a typical example:

After the All Clear, I put in my report to [Air Raid Warden Post] 108D about what had happened to me. I went round to the Alvis and there people were standing outside the ruins. I asked, "What's the score?" and they replied, "Oh, we think there's one or two inside." So I said, "Has anybody been in to see?" and they said, "No, no."

Mr Pratt was the Works Engineer and he told me that nobody was going in, but I said, "Somebody's going in. I'm going in. Anybody coming with me?" Schreiber, one of the Home Guards, Jim Seaman and I went in. We found [–], the nightwatchman. We found part of his leg. That was all there was, with the braid down the trouser leg stuck to it. And we found [–]'s hat and there was somebody else whom we couldn't identify in the Hardening Shop. But, as it happened, [-, the man whose hat they found] was safe. He'd gone home......

Everybody was curious as to what was going to happen to them, so they came and reported [to the Alvis] and were told to come back on the Monday, as there would be some work for them. It wouldn't be their own jobs, of course. So they all came back on the Monday and, by that time, several of us had been instructed, especially the chargehands and myself, to tell them what to do about removing and clearing up the debris.

Well, each was told he would, hopefully, be rehoused in another area, so he could carry on the production he was doing. But nobody knew where he was going and it wasn't for a fortnight or thereabouts that people were told there would be a factory opening in Mount Sorrell [near Loughborough]...... I don't know, possibly over seventy-five per cent of them decided to go to Mount Sorrell.[70]

Arguments in the Council House

I didn't remotely appreciate until I started walking to work the extent of the thing. As I approached the town I jolly soon did. When I got to work at the Council House it was still ablaze, with the fire brigade standing helplessly by because there was no water supply. The first thing we did was to pull down the blackout curtains because we were afraid the flying sparks would cause a fire in the Council House itself.

What struck me most was that people converged on the Council House, despite the devastation and the fact that fires were still raging. It was a very stabilising factor that the Council House was still standing and that there were people in there who were prepared to do what they could to answer questions and give information. Authority seemed to be functioning.

Most of the officers, at least in my department, the Town Clerk's Department, stood about in the corridors answering questions, but I had to attend a meeting which suddenly blew up with the arrival of Herbert Morrison, the Home Secretary, Florence Horsburgh [Parliamentary Secretary to the Ministry of Health], Lord Dudley, the Regional Commissioner, and a whole host of Army, Navy and Airforce brass hats. It really was quite an extraordinary meeting.

Its major decision was to set up an organisation under the chairmanship of Billy [Lord] Rootes to see to the restoration of the gas, water, electricity and transport services, so that, primarily, industry would be able to start to function again for war purposes.

That having been done, there was the other question to be tackled, about how one dealt with the mess we were in. It was a physical mess primarily, but there were the dead to deal with and also the very awkward factor that most of the central shops had been destroyed, in particular the food shops. Everybody's ration cards were related to dealing with a particular shop and, if your shop had disappeared, you weren't rationed with anybody else. So there were a lot of things of that sort which had to be sorted out, but these were sorted out by the local organisation.

A very interesting thing immediately happened. There were a lot of people milling about, brass hats of all sorts and so on, plus the members of the city's Emergency Committee. And one of the admirals said, "Well, I think the Navy is the senior service, and so I'll take the Chair," at which Alderman Halliwell, the Chairman of the Emergency Committee, said, "No, the civil army is still in control here," and sat down in the Chair and opened the meeting. It was, to my mind, an extremely significant thing and it was accepted from then on that, although they were in great need of national help, in fact, the people to run the affair at the end of the day were local people.[120]

Damaged food stores — preliminary estimate

Retail shops:	destroyed	75	
	seriously damaged	125	
	damaged slightly	300	
Warehouses:	destroyed	2	
	damaged	3	
Bakeries:	destroyed	2	
Cafés and restaurants:	destroyed	25	[17]

Nelli Lamberti witnessed the destruction of many shops and had her own house destroyed:

We never got a spoon out of it. We just had what we stood up in, my husband, me and my two girls......

Further up from where we lived there was the pawn shop, Evans', and opposite there Evans had a furniture shop. When the lads that did the fire watching went up that way, to see if people were in the shelter, they found the flames meeting across the road. There were rings, watches, and all sorts of things scattered from the pawn shop window. That night, women were coming down crying because some of them had pawned their husband's suits, unknown to their husbands. Of course, they were hard times, and they were ringing their hands with worry. It was terrible, it was really......

[There were] a lot of people up the street and, in one or two shops in Spon Street, there were people hanging out dead. And when the chaps came and told us, oh dear. At that time we were tearing our petticoats up for bandages. We tore pillow slips up for the people coming in covered in blood. Yes, it was terrible.[84]

Final estimate of shops and food destroyed

The final estimate of shops destroyed shows clearly the devastation wreaked on the city. Eighty per cent of restaurants and teashops were destroyed. provoking a serious shortage of food catering and quick service, at the very time when people were most desperately in need of them. The large daily influx of workers into the city, as well as the building workers and soldiers brought in to repair the damage, added to the problem and stretched the city's unrationed food stocks. The feeling that Coventry was not getting its fair share of food was the result of this acute problem of distribution and the city received special treatment from the Ministry of Food. Rationing was scrapped for a short time, though this actually increased the problem in one way, because outsiders rushed to the city to take advantage. However, emergency canteens were set up and there were a large number of works canteens still functioning.

Food shops:	Pre-blitz	Destroyed	Remaining
Rationed food	1,808	782 (43%)	1,026
Rationed and unrationed food	3,640	1,108 (30%)	2,532
Totals	5,448	1,890 (35%)	3,558
Other shops	1,626	574 (35%)	1,052
All shops	7,074	2,464 (35%)	4,610

Twenty-three out of forty-seven furniture dealers were destroyed, seven out of eleven glass merchants, fourteen out of twenty-nine tobacconists, and twelve out of twenty-two jewellers. There were major shortages of furniture to replace that lost in the raid, glass for broken windows, and replacements for household items such as kitchen utensils, bedding, linoleum, carpets and curtains.[95]

Looting punished

"The magistrates are determined to stop looting," remarked the Chairman (Mrs W E Givens) at Coventry Police Court yesterday [shortly after the raid] in passing a sentence of twenty-eight days' hard labour on an Irish labourer,

John [–] who pleaded guilty to stealing bottles of beer, value 4s 2d, from Messrs C Southern & Co's Windsor Street factory, which had been damaged by war operations.

Detective France said, at 4.30 pm [–] was stopped by a Home Guard and a search revealed five bottles of beer. At the police station the prisoner stated he took the beer to make himself sleep.

The prisoner, who expressed his sorrow, told the court that he was down and out and had had no sleep for two nights.[94]

Looting was a serious problem after the raid. The Chief Constable's report for 1940 lists five hundred and fifty-eight cases, including four hundred and eight from meters and machines. There were a similar number of cases in 1941, but then incidences virtually disappeared. With ruined and evacuated properties everywhere, parentless children wandering the streets, poverty and desperation, people often having lost everything, down to not even a spare pair of socks, temptation was irresistible. Breaking open meters and petty crime were particularly prevalent among the young, including children. Scarce and rationed goods were sometimes stolen as well. Three Salford firemen were convicted of stealing cigarettes, as was a female shop assistant.

City of the dead

17 November 1940

Dear Ber,

When or how you get this letter, I don't know. I've tried to send a telegram, I've tried to telephone, but all to no purpose.

Coventry is a city of the dead, utterly devastated. We have no gas, electric light and, in most cases, no water. We have no milk or bread at the moment. Mobile vans, we hear, are going round the town with bread and water. Loud speakers are going round telling the homeless where to meet to be taken out of the city.

Beryl, it is indescribable. I have not seen a house that has escaped. We are among the lucky ones as we *only* have our windows smashed and part of the roof bashed in. Dad and I were in the cubby hole from 7 pm until 6 am and all the time gun firing and bombs whistling overhead, not a moment's lull. I should think hundreds of planes must have come over and I shall never forget the night of terror. Our knees trembled, we seemed to sit and wait for death as we heard roofs crashing and glass flying. Quite a lot of the greenhouse is broken and our French doors were wrenched open and the back door torn from the lock, but all in Canley Gardens were caused by blasts from bombs that fell in Beechwood Avenue. We had no direct hits.

You remember [–] Cottage where the [–] lived? That and next door have completely vanished and the whole family buried underneath. All those houses in Beechwood Avenue are uninhabitable, also all Rochester Road and, again, I say Earlsdon is lucky. Many land mines must have been used, as whole streets have vanished. There is nothing left of Broadgate, the Cathedral is in ruins, only the spire is left, and that doesn't look safe. The Central Library has gone, the Market Hall has gone, in fact, I think it would be easier to say what hasn't gone.

The centre of the town is roped off, no one is allowed within half a mile of it. There are so many unexploded bombs about, they are talking of blasting the town because none of the buildings seem safe. Mrs Givens has just told me that one can't get near the Council House for people waiting for death certificates and there are still many thousands buried underneath the Market Hall, Owen Owen, and other shelters. None of the factories are working. Everyone seems bewildered. We are indeed a stricken city.

Auntie Amy and family are here. They had incendiary bombs through their roof and were fetched out of the shelter during the raid. Their bed was on fire and they were unable to put the fire out, so the whole lot had to be thrown out of the window. When they did eventually get out of the shelter to their house, they were given ten minutes to get away, because there was an unexploded mine in the vicinity. I don't know how they will be able to go, as there are three large holes in the roof and, to make matters worse, it has been raining quite a lot ever since.

Mrs Randle has had to leave her house; they have gone to Bob's. There isn't a part of the town whole. They must have criss-crossed the city backwards and forwards, dropping bombs at random. It seems a deliberate attempt to smash the city, but why Coventry, I don't know. I have never known so many soldiers. The town is full of them, clearing the debris. The military powers have taken over the city and everyone has to obey orders. In one way, I wish you could see it, but I feel sure it would make you weep. They told us it made the King weep when he saw the devastation. It has to be seen to be believed.

Dunnicliffe said he was going to Leicester yesterday and would try to get a telegram through to you and Bern to assure you we were safe. Then on Sunday afternoon some Rugby friends called to see if we were all right and they offered to send one from Rugby to Bern and he could use a public telephone to let you know. Well, Beryl, we are safe so far and I don't see why we should be afraid now, for there is nothing left for them to bomb now.

I hope you too are safe. We heard that London has been badly hit again, but you see, we have no papers or wireless yet.

Well, I must away. There is much to do.

Very much love from Mum.[4]

158

23 November 1940

Dear Ber,

We received your telegram and express letter yesterday (Friday) evening and I had been very anxiously waiting to hear from you. I hope you have had the telegrams that other people tried to send for us. No telegrams were accepted from this end and, of course, all the wires are down for the telephones.

We are still without gas as many of the mains are broken. We are fortunate as the electricity is working now and, of course, I can cook on the stove, but such a lot have still to cook with fire, as we had to do for several days. Many are still without water.

We have to boil every drop for drinking. The dull, wet November days make our city a city of desolation. You needn't worry about us. We have plenty to eat now: in fact, more than enough. Much food has been rushed into the city and half the population are fleeing from it; then, of course, the death roll is terrible.

You see, Beryl, it started early in the evening and many people were trapped in shelters. We heard that people were alive under the market as late as Thursday, tapping to be released. Owen Owen is to be sealed up and a great many people were buried underneath the crypt of the Cathedral, whose Provost has supported the war effort of Coventry.

Soldiers are everywhere, standing at ends of roads and streets with fixed bayonets, asking your business. Furniture vans are constantly moving people's homes and I saw Walter [–] among the debris of his home, rescuing things. People seem to think Coventry's not a safe place to live anymore, but where is there a safe place?

We did have one quiet night, the night after the raid, but every night since we have had them over, and many times during the day. Last night the sirens went at 7 pm and the All Clear went after Dad and I got up. The night has been a terror. Continual heavy gunfire and hundred of planes soaring over all night long. Where they have been, we don't know yet, but it seems to strike terror into our hearts.

We still have Arthur's family with us. They will go as soon as their roof is on, but when that will be, I don't know, there are so many to do. We haven't been able to get ours done yet, but ours only leaks a bit, so I suppose we must wait our turn, but it is cold and draughty with so many windows bust.

You talk of going to Kenilworth, well Kenilworth is packed with Coventry people and the other night they dropped a land mine in the centre of it......

Hope you are safe and well,

Very much love to you.[4]

159

15 January 1941

Dear Mary and Walter,

Thanks for your kind letter, very pleased to hear that you have had no bombs...... They are funny times we are living in now, we live from day to day......

It was a most dreadful time. We cannot describe it. We were in the shelter from 6.15 at night till 6.30 the next morning and there was not two minutes without bombs and land mines and torpedo bombs. We never thought we could live through it. It was hell let loose and the fires were terrible. It made it worse as they came early and we had not so much as a drop of water in the shelter that night. Other times I take food and the flash in, but all we had time for was a drop of brandy that Dad had slipped in his pocket.

There were eight in the shelter and every time the bombs came, we linked hands and prayed to the God above to save our lives and He answered our prayers. When it was over we could not come out of the shelter as there was a land mine close that had not gone off. We had to stay in the shelter till eleven o'clock in the morning and when we came outside, the windows were all out and the roof all down and most of the doors off. We had to get right away till Tuesday and leave the house as it was. We went to my son's at West Bromwich till Tuesday morning. When we came back, the water had got in and spoilt beds and other things. Dad bought felt and made frames for windows and we got someone to do the roof privately, but we did have to beg so hard. Then we went to some friends at Wellingborough. Dad stayed a week, but I stayed another fortnight, but I could not rest with Dad being alone, so I asked him to fetch me back again.

Mary, I could not sleep while I was away thinking of Bert and they were having gunfire at Coventry all the time. When Dad fetched me back on the Sunday, we had a dreadful night with gunfire again......

When we came out of shelter that morning we had neither water, gas, nor light, but they have been wonderful and they got the gas on for us at Xmas Eve, so we were able to cook our Xmas dinner. We had to boil all water for some time, but now they have got it all right for us......

Mary, we have no big shops now to shop from. We have not seen an onion here and leeks are 6^d for one, not a bunch. They were 6^d a bunch at Wellingborough and apples are 1/6^d at some places, but we are not too bad, considering the way he [Hitler] bombed us out and we are not without food, thanks to our fine lads......

Well, cheerio, all the best......

Ever your friends,

Mr and Mrs Cockerill.[33]

18 November 1940

Dear Maud,

I managed to slip into Coventry this morning on my bicycle and went direct to Wal's office. I am happy to say that, apart from three burnt fingers, Wal is quite well. From the office Wal took me to [–] Park Road. Here we met Janet working away with mop and bucket, trying to clear up. Janet was quite well and for once was too preoccupied to worry about small inconsequentials.

Of the town itself, well, there is no town left. All the shops in the centre are gone. The main streets are hard to find. At least a square mile of the city centre is gutted, and when I say gutted, I mean gutted. Not an article is left in any of the shops, in fact, every shop is burnt out.

Coventry is without electric light, gas, tap water, radio (the radio is on the services system, like electric light), no papers, no post, no telephone system and is a legion of the lost, and indeed they are lost.

Do you know that the raid lasted from 7.10 pm Friday [sic] to 6.40 am Saturday [sic] and at just after 2 am the guns ran out of shells and Jerry just came down to less than fifty feet, only just over the house tops. The first few bombs cut the water mains and the resultant fires just had to burn themselves out. In fact, some were burning this morning [four days after the raid]. I cannot give you a real description, only seeing will convey the disaster.

The ruins are not only in the city centre. Out in the suburbs the damage is almost as bad. On the Birmingham Road the damage reaches out practically until the last house.

I went into Coventry via the back way — Hampton in Arden and Hearsall Common. Here too the damage was just as bad. In one shelter on Hearsall Common eighty people were killed. The papers say two hundred killed, eight hundred injured. No one in Coventry believes these figures.

Wal says that over two thousand have been killed, and the injured beyond the ken of man. You will see in the papers that the people of Coventry are not down-hearted and are giving three cheers at all times of the day — don't believe it!!! If they ever did cheer, then, believe me, they are sick of it and want better and more practical things than fine word speeches and promises and charity from well-meaning, out of work, well-to-dos.

It is said that we English always muddle through to victory. If that is right, then we shall certainly win through this time.

This morning I saw in Coventry, Army brass hats standing on the steps of the ruins of the Midland Bank directing operations......

There are some of these tea vans going about giving cups of tea away, but what are wanted are plenty of the travelling shops, because people do not want charity while they have money in their pockets. Also, what is wanted is a local news sheet printed in a motor van, if necessary, giving information to the homeless and not bellowing at the poor devils through megaphones. Nobody ever knew what a megaphone had said anyway.

The Birmingham Co-op has sent eight thousand loaves and gallons of fresh, clean water.

I do not think it will be much use you writing to Wal for a day or two, everything is in so much of a muck, with not a post office and hardly a pillar box left.

The house next to Wal's was burnt right out. About six houses right opposite were bombed right out and further down the road about twenty houses were also bombed right out.

Wal's house is not too bad. Most of the tiles are gone and each room lets in water, excepting the kitchen.

Wal does not know what will happen at his office. The building is still there (only just), but most of the papers have gone, burnt out. He says that they will stay on as best they can and see what turns up.

I have asked them to come to us and, if the office is split up and parts sent to Birmingham, Leamington, Warwick, then I have no doubt that Wal and Janet will come to us.

By the way, Wal and Janet had a delayed action bomb just outside their house and were evacuated, but dodged back via the entry and slept in their kitchen.

I have gone over to see Dad and tell him the news.

Pleased to know that you are well and cheerful. Can't write much more now. Jerry is very low over our house right now.

Love Dick

PS Jerry now dropping land mines on parachutes, also exploding incendiaries, so don't dash out too soon with your buckets of sand.[12]

The King!

I was in Hay Lane, by the corner of Anslows. There was a queue of people trying to get some news of relatives who were dead or missing.

Without any warning, the King suddenly appeared, in Army uniform. He was walking with a group of people and I always remember a bus conductor who climbed a gas lamp post and clung onto it and waved his hat in the air, shouting, "Three cheers for King George!"

It was quite marvellous! [28]

His Majesty the King visited the city on 16 November and stood within the ruins of the Cathedral. There, speaking for the whole country and people, he expressed his deep sorrow at the scene of destruction upon which he gazed. Royalty had visited St Michael's on several occasions in its past history, but surely never was there such a visit as this.[32]

King George VI and Queen Elizabeth return to the Cathedral in 1942

The khaki clad officer with the red banded cap of the "brass hat" was standing near St John's Church in Holyhead Road two days after the November blitz. There was a dark coloured car close at hand.

I was curious. I propped my bicycle against a convenient pile of debris, sidled up to a police sergeant and asked, "Sarge, who's the staff officer?"

"Staff officer be — , that's the King."

The King turned round. He was carrying a small cane with which he had been prodding something in the wreckage nearby. He had previously had his back to me and had probably overheard the little conversation. He came back slowly towards us, placing his cane under his arm.

I didn't know what to do. As I was bareheaded, with my helmet strapped to my bike, I came smartly to attention. The King halted a yard in front of me and stood looking at me. No word was spoken. I thought, surely protocol demands that he speak first. We simply stood and looked at each other. I tried to convey silently how sorry I felt that he should have come to Coventry and seen the city in such a state. I felt that we had lost most of the city we knew, but that he was concerned with the welfare and security, not only of Coventry, but of the Empire.

All these thoughts passed through my mind, together with noticing how tired and weary he looked. Suddenly, the King glanced at his wristwatch, turned to the sergeant, motioned him to follow, and walked slowly away to the car. Both men climbed in and drove away.

It was only much later that I formed the opinion that the King had chosen to spend a few minutes' silence with us.[51]

No King was ever more a man among his people than King George VI when he came to Coventry on Saturday and for four hours made Coventry's sorrows his own. [NB Queen Elizabeth — our present Queen Mother — came too] It may well be that never in the whole history of the British monarchy has a royal visit proved more of a tonic to a suffering people — nor left behind more inspiration for the gigantic task of restoring order out of chaos.

The King walked for miles around the shattered districts of the city, accompanied by Mr Herbert Morrison (Home Secretary and Minister for Home Security), who had also made Coventry's problems his personal affair.

His Majesty tramped through streets deep in mud and rubble and climbed over piles of debris. He wanted first-hand information and he got it......

The Mayor, Alderman J A Moseley met the King and drove with him to the Council House which, though damaged, remained one of the few central buildings capable of occupation. Visiting first the Cathedral ruins, His Majesty spent some time amid the heaps of debris between the walls of the building. Slabs of masonry lay on all sides; nothing remained but the famous tower and spire and the four gaunt walls.

The King saw other parts of the city centre which were in ruins and then was taken by car to St George's Church, Radford, which had been converted into a rest centre, because the church hall had been struck. Amid the beds which crowded the aisles, the King spoke to numerous people who had been bombed out of their homes and had lost their every possession.

The King's emotion was apparent, and his obvious deep feeling for the sufferings of his people touched all who saw him. At St George's, the King spoke words of encouragement to many elderly folk who had found refuge there. These included Mr and Mrs Tate, Mrs Ruth Lewis, who is seventy-eight years of age, and Mrs Margaret Allbutt, who is seventy-five. The King also spoke to the Reverend G L Bennett, curate at the church, who had welcomed His Majesty and, as he passed on to view other parts of the city, all present in the church joined in singing the National Anthem.

Later, the King stopped at the home of the Mayor in Kensington Road, which had also been damaged during the night. As he left someone shouted, "Are we downhearted?" and the King joined in the cry of, "No!"

The King continued his tour for hours and saw the whole scene of devastation before returning to the Council House. Throughout, the King rarely missed speaking to a Civil Defence worker with whom it was possible to have a word as he passed by. This personal consideration of them, and thanks for the work they were doing, was as expressive as anything in the visit.

Finally, he summed up his impressions by saying to Mr Herbert Morrison, "I'm so glad things have gone so well in these dreadful circumstances."

The King took lunch with other members of the Royal Party, including Mr Morrison, Miss Florence Horsburgh, Parliamentary Secretary to the Ministry of Health, and Lord Dudley, Regional Commissioner for Civil Defence. However, much to the delight of the crowds, His Majesty set out for another extended tour on foot. By a roundabout route he got eventually to Pool Meadow when AFS men were being fed at several mobile canteens. His Majesty spoke with several men as they were taking this brief respite from long hours of duty.

The King several times expressed interest in the welfare of out-of-town fighting units which had been drafted into the city to give assistance and provide relief for the local fire servicemen. He was told that large armies of helpers from outside areas were brought into the city while the raid was in progress.

The King had a long talk with Alderman W E Halliwell, Chairman of the War Emergency Committee. Before he left, the King stood outside the Council House chatting earnestly with the Mayor, Lord Dudley, Mr Morrison, the Chief Constable, and others. He was overheard to remark that he was satisfied everything possible was being done for the welfare of the people of Coventry.[94]

The King wrote in his diary that he had found the Emergency Committee "quite dazed" by the blitz:

I walked among the devastation. The people in the streets wondered where they were — nothing could be recognised......The old part of the town looks just like Ypres after the last war.   [8]

Reprise

The extent of the devastation in Coventry the morning after the blitz was staggering, as this list of houses damaged and destroyed, district by district, from figures in the City Archives, shows:

House damage, by district

	Totally Destroyed	Demolition Necessary	Seriously Damaged	Evacuated	Slight Damage
Earlsdon	22	30	308	—	2280
Spencer Park	—	29	405	103	374
Green Lane	10	24	128	115	536
Greyfriars(1)	57	92	103	91	1035
Allesley Old Road	3	36	360	111	1491
Hill St/Barras Lane	61	191	465	524	132
Widdrington Road	49	116	153	196	770
Allesley	10	9	439	206	1992
Coundon	33	23	866	217	103
Keresley	—	15	50	79	1269
Daimler	19	61	631	412	1496
Courtaulds	4	12	133	54	330
Eagle Street	74	125	584	455	817
Holbrooks(West)	12	8	88	120	544
Holbrooks(East)	29	31	155	152	1400
Foleshill Gas Works	7	147	130	130	1075
Longford	—	—	51	12	413
Old Church Road	1	14	282	82	929
Alderman's Green	—	4	48	2	329
Rover Works	50	161	857	227	567
Courthouse Green	—	14	31	58	832
Ordnance Works	25	41	242	145	682
Stoke Heath	19	41	692	103	423
Caludon Castle	8	8	131	53	812
Hillfields	104	88	1435	816	351
Wyken	28	87	658	447	1181
Far Gosford Street	20	154	482	209	518

Stoke Park	3	9	240	62	1210
Humber	32	24	222	95	1628
Copsewood	6	7	191	38	824
Cheylesmore	8	43	94	42	2277
Whitley	3	9	43	15	73
Tile Hill	—	—	—	2	149
Canley	—	—	—	—	4
Hearsall	2	5	42	20	152
Greyfriars(2)	20	20	95	48	249
Stivichall	2	7	26	6	158
	721	1,570	10,908	5,447	29,705

From these statistics, we can see that the areas which bore the brunt of the attack were Hillfields, the areas around the Daimler like Eagle Street and Widdrington Road, and the city centre (Greyfriars). The suburbs were not badly hit, with houses destroyed, but some suffered worse than the inner city in respect of overall numbers of houses damaged. In the case of Cheylesmore and Earlsdon, this was because they were on the bombers' approach routes. Five and a half thousand families had to be evacuated, a huge number, whilst nearly two thousand three hundred houses were destroyed or had to be demolished. A further eleven thousand were seriously damaged and some thirty thousand slightly damaged. The total number of houses damaged and destroyed ran to 42,904. Out of a total housing stock of seventy-five thousand, this amounted to fifty-six per cent.

The number of deaths has always been a matter of conjecture and seems surprisingly low. As noted on page eighty, among the factors possibly responsible that numerous witnesses mention was that several public shelters were filled in without the bodies being taken out, as all were known to be dead inside.

I remember the air raid shelters that they just sealed off due to everyone there being dead. One that I can recall was at the bottom of Hertford Street where the Three Tuns is situated now. Although hundreds died in the diabolic blitzes in Coventry...... a lot more died without being counted.[110]

Another important factor was that no patients were killed in the hospitals, the only fatality being a soldier standing in the grounds of the Coventry and Warwickshire Hospital. The morning after the raid, 260 patients were evacuated, partly with the help of an entire fleet of American ambulances:

Coventry and Warwickshire Hospital sustained very intensive damage early in the November blitz and, of course, the burden of the work for the rest of the period of that awful night was undertaken by Gulson Hospital and we were evacuating patients after treatment, probably within twelve hours after the blitz. We were evacuating by the following morning after the blitz. We started evacuating patients to Rugby, Solihull and various hospitals around the Midlands from about eleven o'clock in the morning...... There were buses and ambulances specially fitted out to deal with these types of casualties.[48]

Warning posters were put up everywhere, warning people to boil drinking water, not to use damaged toilets, to bury their own refuse and, despite wrecked sewage systems (one estimate is of over a thousand damaged branch sewers) and polluted water, no epidemics broke out. In fact, as reported by Arthur Massey, Medical Officer of Health, the city's Emergency Medical Service worked smoothly:

At the time of the air attacks, damage to drainage communications and water mains was extensive and the typhoid hazard was real. Preventative measures included (a) intensive local propaganda — by press, posters and Ministry of Information loudspeaker vans — urging the boiling of drinking water and milk; (b) chlorination of water supplies; (c) facilities for anti-typhoid inoculation; and (d) steps to secure the early restoration of water pipes, sewers and drains. On each occasion, the position was quickly cleaned up and no typhoid cases attributable to the air raid conditions did in fact occur.[90]

Arthur Massey did admit, however, that there were serious risks associated with mass evacuation, shelter life, and overcrowded billets:

On the black side are the increased incidence of venereal diseases and phthisis [wasting away of the body], housing shortage and domestic overcrowding.

Special inoculation clinics were set up, as well as a Mobile Inoculation Unit. 20,000 people were treated. Showers at public places and factories where the water supply was clean were opened to the public. One major effect of the raid was to greatly increase the number of people leading a "shelter life" which caused more problems of hygiene and, by April 1941, there was a major problem of rat infestation. Arthur Massey also mentions mental health as a problem, once more giving a different picture to the official "We can take it" line, as people suffered from shock, depression and a sense of hopelessness.

Of the Coventry and Warwickshire Hospital, severly damaged in the raid, there was only space left for a hundred beds. However:

On the whole, the health account is in credit. In regard to the city's vicissitudes through enemy bombing, some compensation is to be found in the enormous opportunity now afforded for bold and healthy town planning. The City Council is not likely to lose this chance of a future Coventry on model lines.[90]

Kenneth Turner, of the Town Clerk's Department, had to deal with the task of identifying and dealing with hundreds of dead bodies in the mortuaries:

There was a mortuary established in Hill Street to which all the bodies collected from under the debris had been taken and the idea was that relatives should be able to go there and identify the dead and satisfy themselves in that way. Unfortunately, the mortuary itself was also bombed and a state of chaos was rendered even more chaotic.

Three or four days after the raid, the Medical Officer of Health, who was responsible for the mortuary, and the Chief Constable, who was in charge of public morale, had a serious difference of opinion. The Chief Constable was saying that, unless people could go to the mortuary and identify the dead, there would be riots and trouble, and the Medical Officer of Health was saying that conditions at the mortuary were such that it was impossible for anyone to do this.

They came to consult the Town Clerk and he asked me to go and inspect the mortuary and give my opinion of it. He sent me off with a bottle of whisky in my pocket to sustain me and, indeed, when I got there I found I needed it.

The mortuary staff were engaged in fitting bits and pieces together to make whole bodies and, in many cases, there was no means of identification or anything of that sort. The whole place was, literally, a shambles.

I came out and stood on a box at the entrance to the gas works and a crowd of about two or three hundred had gathered. I said I'd been in and made an inspection, and that it was not possible for them to go in. That led to great shouts, and so on, in particular from some service chaps in the front row who had been allowed home on compassionate leave. I picked a sailor and an airman from the crowd and said, "You can come in," and took them inside.

They were both violently sick within a couple of minutes. They came outside and said, "It's right, what he says," and the crowd accepted it and dispersed.

After this, people couldn't arrange for private burials — it would have been impossible for four or five hundred individual graves to have been dug and, of course, they couldn't choose which was their body out of all these. So it was decided and accepted that the whole lot be buried in a mass grave.[120]

As the long queue of relatives stretched outside the Council House for news of loved ones, the appalling work of identification went on. Rumours spread of mass produced coffins. Public baths were being used as emergency mortuaries and arrangements were made at the London Road Cemetery for the mass graves — two long, parallel trenches — and the two funeral services.

The bodies were put into shrouds and taken to the cemetery on the nights preceding the services. All were in coffins, many of which were brought in from neighbouring cities to cope with the numbers required. At 11 am on the dull, grey morning of 19 November, the first service was held. [The second was four days later.] No general announcement of the service was made and fighter planes were sent up against possible air attacks from the Germans:

The service for the Anglicans and Free Churchmen was to be a combined one, preceded by a short service conducted by the Roman Catholic priests. The graves were two deep and long trenches, into which the rough and unpolished oak coffins had been placed during the previous night. Here and there a Union Jack was spread over the open graves. In the background stood the mechanical trench-digger and groups of soldiers and labourers who had been working throughout the night at the grim task of carrying the coffins and lowering them into the graves.

At the time for the beginning of the service, preparations were not complete...... When all was ready, we moved in order towards the gate to meet the crowd of mourners, who were led up the road through the cemetery by a contingent of police, firemen and wardens. Then, at the top of the rise, the Bishop and clergy, followed by the civic officials, took the lead to the graveside. It was a quiet and solemn procession. The soft beat of the rubber boots of the firemen, the measured tread of the police and wardens, marching in step across the gravel path, seemed to accentuate the silence. In the distance, against the grey, scudding sky, a Spitfire wheeled and twisted; the sound of its engine came fitfully to us down the wind. Pressmen and press photographers, both for the newspapers and newsreels, hurried here and there. A distasteful task this, I reflected — like photographing Calvary!

At the graveside it was possible to turn and look back over the long line of mourners still approaching. It was a pathetic sight: women carrying wreaths; here and there a child with a bunch of flowers; the black suits and dresses relieved occasionally by a splash of colour of the uniform of a husband, a son, or a brother on compassionate leave. It seemed as if there was no end to this long, dark line which moved slowly across the grass. At last the great crowd was gathered around the graves.

The Roman Catholic priest stepped forward and, hardly lifting his eyes from his book, read the service. Men and women in the crowd knelt on the grass or clay and crossed themselves and murmured with him the Paternoster.

Then the Bishop and the Free Church minister appointed for the task stepped forward......

The service over, the Mayor, carrying a wreath, led the mourners up and down the gravesides and, as they followed, they laid their wreaths and dropped their posies and sprays into the graves. Some peered anxiously at the bloodstained labels attached to the coffins to see if, perchance, they could see the name of their relative or friend. Most of the names were (perhaps fortunately) indecipherable.

At last, some hurried away, although some still lingered at the graveside.

The clergy and ministers moved in and out among them, speaking words of comfort to the distressed and seeking out members of their own congregations.

It was with that picture in my mind that I turned away from that sad scene with the words ringing in my ears: "In the midst of life we are in death. I am the Resurrection and the Life, saith the Lord. He that believeth in Me, though he were dead, yet shall he live."[35]

How welcome good cups of tea served by the mobile canteens were!

Many of the five and a half thousand homeless families evacuated, were first given clothes and meals at the rest centres and public canteens. By 18 November, all children of school age, plus their teachers, were called upon for immediate evacuation. The report of the Civil Defence force states that 2,200 people had been evacuated or rehoused by 26 November.

The report also mentions that twenty thousand blankets had been brought up by special train from London, with a further twelve thousand coming from the West Midlands region. It does state that *provision* was made to evacuate ten thousand people. However, only three hundred and fifty-seven turned up. "The inhabitants prefered to stay where they were and, if they did take part in a daily evacuation scheme of their own, they duly returned."

The WVS cared for those devastated:

Perhaps there is no more distressing a sight than that of tired, hungry and homeless women and children wandering hopelessly about amid desolation and ruin; and the care and attention lavished on these unfortunate people by the WVS was an inspiration to all.[73]

Me, my mother and sister returned home at last over the debris. Destruction was all around. On both sides of the road stood the shells of former home-steads, many still burning. One end of our street was devastated, the result of a landmine. We walked over the door into what was left of our house, then waited for my father and brother to return. It was agony to see the sun rising and them not returning, but it was a prayer answered when they walked into the house safe and sound.

With the sun and daylight there also came fresh vapour trails. The Germans were taking photographs of the havoc they had wrought. Coventry was more or less out of action. Food was brought in from other towns and the homeless were given clothing and shelter in rest centres. With the water supply gone, we depended on the contents of our rainwater butt until the Council got the water wagons moving. In the winter cold, the WVS vans brought us meals and we soldiered on beneath tarpaulin covered roofs and boarded up windows.

The only thing that really mattered was that the family was safe and we were together. In time, the factory chimneys smoked again and the women who withstood the air attacks from Germany helped in the factories to make guns, planes and shells to prevent more bombing and destruction over the shores of England.[128]

The damage to the infrastructure affected the bakeries, which had to stop baking because of polluted water. Several had been completely knocked out of action. Messengers were despatched to other towns and thousands of loaves poured in, especially from Birmingham, to fulfill the daily require-ments of 60,000 to 80,000 loaves. 421,000 were received up to 22 December. One of Sutton's bakeries on the outskirts of the city survived and ran on one clean main, a temporary power supply and superhuman efforts by the workforce. It produced 12,000 loaves a day, but:

This figure, in cold print, gives little indication of the difficulties overcome, and of the almost superhuman endurance of those engaged. At one period men carried on working for twenty-six hours without respite,......innumerable cups of tea, prepared by girls in the office, being carried to them as they worked.[3]

However, even with this bakery, the city received only half its normal supply of loaves over the next month, though the report states that "no one went without bread". Perhaps that shows how many people had been evacuated or had left the city.

Water tankers were to become a regular sight on the city's streets as well. All fresh meat was taken out of the city to be destroyed. Frozen meat was ruined, as refrigeration systems broke down with the loss of electricity. Many lost their ration books, so free food was made available from mobile canteens for a few days. Seven thousand tarpaulins were handed out to patch holes in roofs and the Mayor's Fund for the Relief of Air Raid Distress helped those who had lost their furniture and possessions.

Nor did the animals escape. The People's Dispensary For Sick Animals dealt with over nine hundred animals in the two weeks after the raid.

Between December 1940 and January 1941, the population of the city, estimated at 260,000 prior to the blitz, fell to 210,000, though it had risen rapidly back again by February. Obviously, people were evacuated, but then returned to the city as quickly as they could once basic services had been restored and repairs made.

The banks and building societies had to deal with pressing financial problems. The Coventry Building Society tried to help the homeless mortgage payers as best it could and some of the letters it was sent by distraught customers are very distressing:

Our house...... is quite destroyed by fire of incendiary bombs. My sons tried their best to put it out but it was hopeless...... Our house in Thornhill is not habitable and there are two unexploded bombs in the back garden so the police turned us out, and we had nowhere in Coventry to go; the Germans have just about finished us.[42]

The trek of evacuees from the city continued over the weekend and into the following week. Every available car, bus, cart, pram and bicycle was heavily laden with dusty, assorted possessions. The appeal for shelter went out to all of the local towns in Warwickshire.

Kenilworth, Leamington, Rugby, Nuneaton and Stratford all took their share, people often walking the entire distance. Billetting Officers in these towns made provision, though the greatest strain was on Leamington and Kenilworth which, together, took in 1,500 people, many into public halls and rest centres. All were fed and given warm shelter and plenty of sympathy.

Amazingly, workers who had spent the night outside the city arrived the morning after the raid anxious to get back to work. Their attitude was defiant and one of wanting to get on with the job, even if it was only clearing up. This attitude was reflected in the officials as well.

Getting war production going again became the number one priority. This was clear from the report Lord Rootes produced on the lesson of the raid. Factories were rapidly brought back into action. Take, for example, the

Alvis, which was the scene of blazing fires and torrents of incendiaries and high explosives:

Although the buildings of the Car Department were totally destroyed, substantial property, plant and machinery was recovered, [they salvaged half of the machine tools there, eventually] together with some part of the stocks contained in that department...... The Aero Engine Repair Department had also suffered damage, mainly to the buildings, although this was not of so severe a nature as in the Car Department...... The position in the Aero Engine Machine Shop was much more satisfactory, damage being slight and...... production had recommenced within two days of the restoration [of essential services] and now approached normal.[2]

Rescue, bomb disposal and demolition work went on day and night. People coped by making tea and rescuing clothes and furniture, though many were clearly badly shaken. One eyewitness records the scene in those chaotic days:

The city was the scene of all kinds of activity: firemen doing what they could with a meagre water supply to keep important administrative buildings from catching fire; lorry loads of soldiers hurrying into the city to assist the police and rescue work; bomb disposal squads locating and dealing with delayed action bombs; buses gathering at various points for the evacuation of children; all kinds of kitchen vans serving out cups of tea and soup and sandwiches; homeless people carrying a few belongings, picking their way through the maze of hoses and over the debris, making for the roads to the south and north, to try and find some country cottage in which they could lodge and rest for a while.[88]

Clearing the streets was soon achieved and some buses ran, though the trams were never to run again after that night. Communications were difficult for several days, but papers rapidly began to arrive, and news was relayed over loudspeaker vans or filtered through somehow.

After the raid, most of the lower part of the city was without running water, whilst the higher levels were still supplied from the Meriden reservoir. It was water from the Coundon reservoir to the lower end of the city which suffered from burst mains. Assistance was drafted in from water authorities as far away as Worcester and they relayed over a mile of piping in restoring two hundred and forty-four damaged sections. A further five and a half miles of temporary mains were also laid, with the assistance of the infantry and Pioneers.

There was great concern over contamination, so the water supply was chlorinated, announcements were made in the local press about the need to boil all drinking water and the previously mentioned anti-typhoid inoculation programme was carried out. The destruction of the old Technical College during the raid destroyed the Water Department's chemical laboratory, drawing office, new supplies office and other offices, together with files, supplies and records. However, within a few days, most areas of the city had their water supply restored. [125]

Emergency petrol coupons were issued to selected drivers. Food was available free for a few days and two cheap municipal cafeterias were soon in operation. A huge supply of canned meat was brought into the city. Food shelters in Worcestershire, Nottinghamshire and Leicestershire were opened up to Coventry evacuees. A number of field kitchens were set up and played an important role in supplying hot meals. Stocks of food, according to the Civil Defence Report, were plentiful.

Could the fires have been prevented?

The Chief Fire Officer, in his report on the raid, felt there was nothing substantial which could have been done to improve the preparedness and equipment of the fire service. The inability to fight the fires was, in his opinion, not due to bad organisation, but to the loss of the water supply, plus the intensity of the raid:

I have carefully reviewed the events of that night and, although the new experience will serve in good stead for the future, I do not feel that many major changes are called for in the local organisation. All pre-arranged plans were brought into action, but the fierceness of the attack and the absence of a single lull seriously hampered our efforts, particularly in assembling and re-disposing of our resources.

Private fire brigades
It is gratifying to note that the factories and premises which were not so seriously damaged by fire were mostly firms which had trained fire brigades or well trained fire watcher parties. These firms really helped themselves without waiting for or depending entirely upon the local authority's resources......

Fire watchers
The fire watchers scheme was eminently successful in some premises, of which the Council House and Trinity Church are two examples. Although hit by incendiary bombs, both of these buildings remain almost intact amidst areas that are otherwise devastated...... The explosive incendiary was undoubtedly the cause of much trouble. During previous raids the proportion of incendiaries to explosive incendiaries had been about ten to one; on this night the proportions were about equal. It was the first local experience of this bomb in

such large numbers and soon resulted in *every* incendiary being treated with the utmost respect. This was particularly the case when it was found that the two types were being dropped mixed together.

He did, however, point to the need for more static water supplies, as mobile fire hydrants had not been able to negotiate cratered roads and had soon exhausted their supply of petrol, a serious and worrying deficiency. Of the regional assistance, whilst he recognised it as inadequate on the night of the big raid, it was because of the speed of the raid's build-up rather than any other factor.[27]

However, one significant improvement as a result of the raid was the introduction, directly out of the Coventry experience, of a national fire service to replace the regional services.

The report by the Civil Defence region on the raid also stated that the main problem was the intensity of the raid, with bombs having "rained in torrents". But the fire service had worked well and the rescue parties in the region had responded adequately, although their equipment and "technical direction" had proved inadequate:

Provided that the damage in any one place is no greater than that experienced in Coventry, and that this damage is only sustained in one, or at most two, towns in the region, it has been proved that the drafting into the city of parties from other parts of the region has been sufficient to meet all requirements.[31]

Fifty-two rescue parties from the region attended at Coventry, with a further twelve from other regions.

The tramway service ceased on the night of 14/15 November 1940, never to run again. The track was destroyed in eleven places, thirty-eight overhead poles were damaged, four and a half miles of trolley wire were brought down and six trams damaged. Whilst the estimated time to repair these was five months, buses ran the routes instead. But the bus service hadn't escaped lightly. Six buses had been totally wrecked, thirteen more needed major rebuilding, thirty-four had suffered major damage, and a further hundred and three had windows broken, a total of a hundred and fifty-six out of a fleet of a hundred and eighty-one.

During all the raids on Coventry, 4,187 school places were destroyed by enemy action, whilst 1,284 had already been lost by the need to build air raid shelters in school grounds. Together with the loss of housing, factories and public buildings, the repairs required were gargantuan. Yet up to five hundred houses were repaired a day, until, by 28 December, 16,048 had been restored and, by 30 January, two thirds (about 28,000) had been restored. Within weeks, a camp for two thousand building workers had been built, although there was still need for accommodating a further six thousand. Materials were salvaged from collapsed factories, where jigs, spare parts and materials had often escaped the worst of the damage.

The Emergency Committee called for improvements in security and fire fighting techniques and considered billetting the huge influx of workers in partially occupied or empty properties. One problem was that many larger buildings had been taken over by anti-aircraft guns and barrage balloons. Transport became a major headache, with blocked roads, smashed railway lines, licencing formalities, and the need to move around repair workers, soldiers and other emergency personnel.

Certainly, the committee began to prepare its defences far more comprehensively after the raid. Another emergency mortuary was established on land owned by the Coventry Motor Mart, two thousand more auxiliary fire service personnel were demanded, at full workingmen's wages. It required the establishment of area camps with sleeping and feeding provision, where reinforcements and equipment could be accommodated. More communal kitchens were to be set up and more hospital places supplied outside the city boundaries.

It also severely criticised the quality of the surface shelters. They had been built with lime mortar to save on cement, suffered from shoddy workmanship, and had proved to be flimsy and totally inadequate.

People suffered from two contradictory, but both very worrying, concerns regarding furniture. For those who had been bombed and had their furniture ruined, but who still had a dwelling of some sort to live in, there was an acute shortage of replacement items. Most of the furniture salvaged from previous raids and stored in the city had been destroyed in the raid, as well as many of the city's furniture and secondhand shops.

Meanwhile, many people who had been completely bombed out, or who had decided to evacuate or move in with family, friends or neighbours, found that their furniture could not be moved into safe keeping. Yet it had to be stored somewhere. For the Emergency Committee, the experience of the raid, which had destroyed several furniture warehouses located in the city, meant furniture had to be stored outside the city, in nearby towns and villages. However, this made it an almost impossible task for people trying to refind their possessions:

Almost daily, people who have had their furniture put in store, perhaps only a few days previously, come along and ask if they can have access to their furniture to retrieve a bank book, a summer dress, or even tinned food which had been left in a cupboard. It can be imagined how difficult this sort of thing can become when, in addition to meeting the seekers at the various stores, the staff must be found to receive and inventory furniture which is being taken into yet another store. The inventories of furniture taken into storage are made in triplicate. One copy is deposited with the furniture, one sent to the owner, and the third kept for office use...... Storage accommodation is so limited and the demand after a heavy raid so great as to make it imperative for people to get their furniture out of store as quickly as possible.[30]

There was frequent criticism of and frustration felt at the lack of official help and organisation. Nelli Lamberti was both critical and thankful after the raid. Officials were not very sympathetic and gave her no help with rehousing after her home was destroyed. People:

had to go into lodgings or do the best they could. Some people managed to go into the country. Perhaps they had got someone living Kenilworth way, or Warwick, or somewhere like that. They did escape a lot of it. We had to stay put......

Help was only given:

now and again. When the blitz was on during the day we used to have what we called the "vittal van". The vans came up with hot soup and tea and dished it out to people who wanted it, and sandwiches and that, you know, all rough. But we were all glad of it, you know.[84]

The minutes of the Coventry Committee of the Ministry of Information make clear the problems of coping with the human costs of the raid. Furniture removal, storage, and retrieval were major concerns. Worry was also expressed, in its 21 January 1941 report, about press reports on how Coventry was "going ahead" after the raid, as if ready to take another pounding. It also states:

Owing to the unpreparedness for such a raid, many lessons had been learned by other towns and cities in the country, and special machinery had been devised which gave a basic standing for the future and which is operating very well.

On public morale, it stated:

It is perfectly wonderful the way in which people have stood up to the test of the 14 November "blitzkrieg". Much disquietude over the fact that people are leaving their premises at night, as this may mean danger to those who remain. More information is wanted by people who have suffered loss. Suggest that each member of the Information Committee has a form such as is issued for the Mayor's Fund For Air Raid Distress, so that they may be in a position to advise persons seeking advice.

Public morale is high, particularly so when food conditions ruling at the moment are taken into account. Food is causing a certain amount of anxiety. Prices are high for commodities not controlled and controlled commodities seem to disappear with the control of price......

Reaction to current news
It is felt that ministers' observations re bombed areas should not be broadcast or printed in such a manner that it invites the enemy to come and finish what he has already started. No statement is preferable to over-statement.

Questions agitating local opinion

Why are bombed out people being asked to pay the expenses of removal? Should not this be a government liability?

Is the Local Information Committee necessary, seeing that its members were not consulted during the worst period in living memory?......

The question of billetting and accommodation for armament workers in the city is causing much anxiety. The constant sight of men seeking lodgings trailing around the city is doing nobody any good......

Since before the raid, Coventrians had felt they were not receiving their fair share of foodstuffs. Despite official assurances that there was plenty of food in the city, this became more acute after the raid. By February 1941, the Committee reported that people were still complaining at the amount of queueing they had to do and that there were no oats, cheese, golden syrup, biscuits, sauces or tinned milk. Items like fruit, eggs and onions vanished as soon as they appeared.

The committee also recommended a series of new measures to be taken in the event of further heavy air raids on the city. They involved setting up a Central Information Office, improving co-ordination between the various local and national agencies and the emergency services, increasing the information available to the public after a raid, special passes for committee members and communicating news to the public. Morale, it was reported, was "at a very high standard at the moment".

Condolences and salutes

As soon as the news of the devastation reached other cities and countries, messages of condolence and support came rushing in:

20 November 1940

Private

My dear Mr Mayor,

I am commanded by The Queen to write and tell you that Her Majesty is sending a consignment of blankets to you for distribution among the homeless, and also under separate cover, a parcel of children's jerseys, etc.

I am to express to you The Queen's deepest sympathy, and to tell you that the people of Coventry are never out of Her Majesty's thoughts.

Marion Hyde,
Lady-in-Waiting [72]

Mr Emil Davies, chairman of the LCC [London County Council] has tele-graphed the Mayor of Coventry that the people of London "salute the people of Coventry for their proud spirit and high courage, and invite the Mayor to let London know if we can be of assistance".[94]

The story of Coventry's tribulation has crossed the high seas and has brought an appreciated response from the city's name ship. The signal received by the Mayor from the Commanding Officer of HMS Coventry is one that reflects the city's growing anger at the dastardly and indescriminate nature of the Nazi attack.

"The complement of HMS Coventry expresses sympathy with the citizens in their adversity and assures them that the ship will endeavour to repay," her commander wired.[94]

The *St Louis Globe Democrat* reported the raid and "the smouldering ruins of Coventry". The *Cleveland Plain Dealer* was horrified at "Coventry's sorrow", whilst the *New York Herald Tribune* stated scathingly:

For the sick and helpless anger which such a spectacle evokes there is but one answer. No means of defence which the United States can place in British hands should be withheld, no effort which this country and every individual can make to stop this horror while still confined beyond the seas is too great to make.

The *New York Times* also reported on the dire situation Britain now seemed to be in and the need to help her out.

These are just a few of the hundreds of messages of sympathy which came from towns and cities across Britain, and individuals, newpapers and governments across the world, and which, in turn, were beamed to the people of the city.

One development which did take place as a direct result of the raid, and surprisingly rapidly after it, was the creation of the City Redevelopment Committee, set up on 10 December 1940. It was required to consider "both in broad outline and in detail the steps which it is desirable for the municipality to take to secure a worthy replanning and redevelopment of the city". By February, just three months after the blitz, it came up with a rec-ommended scheme:

With a square mile of city in which to rebuild, the authorites were faced with two possible solutions. The old street plan could be used a a foundation. If this were done some of the worst streets could be widened, and historical gems such as Ford's Hospital could be retained......[There would be] two main blocks flanking a shopping avenue from which only pedestrians would have access to the recessed arcades. Service roads, approach roads and parking areas are planned at the backs of the shopping blocks and off the main thoroughfares......

Chief amongst these factors [in the plan] is the provision of open space.......Here are the main points of the new plan as set out by the architect:

The increase of aerial transport, particularly passenger transport, after the war, must be borne in mind......Provision has been made for linking up the existing facilities with the centre of the town.

Road and rail transport are governing factors. The railway station on the new plan occupies the same position as the existing station and is coupled with a coach station.

In the central area motor transport and parking have been carefully thought out so that through traffic will be unhampered by local traffic. Parking and service to the shopping centre has received special consideration.

An embryo plan exists showing radial and ring roads in the area outside the city centre, but this need only be taken into consideration at the present time in so far as it affects the feeding and clearance of the centre. Its final lay-out depends on the location of existing property, which might stand for fifty years......The recreation area is treated in a similar way. The cinemas and theatres, generally speaking, are now situated to the north of the shopping district. In the new design they are simply co-ordinated to take their place in, and contribute to, the design as a whole. The hotels are grouped in what would form two fine blocks facing onto Broadgate. [88]

This plan was to be the first of many civic developments which took place throughout the country, in cities which were heavily bombed. It had the first planned central precinct in the country, and was to prove an exciting and influential development. Out of the ashes of the terrible destruction of the blitz rose the phœnix of a new and proud city. As we walk through the city centre, let us not forget the price we have paid for it.

Bibliography of contributors

1 "A" Company, Nᵒ 2 Battalion Home Guard*"Report on Events on and Following 14/15 November 1940"*

2 Alvis *"Minutes of Board Meeting, 12th December 1940"*

3 Author unknown *"A Loaf of Bread"* Report on bread supplies after the air raid of 14/15 November 1940.

4 Author unknown Letters dated 17 and 23 November 1940.

5 Author unknown *"Daimler"* Personal account.

6 Author unknown *"Kingfield Under Fire (1940–1941)"* passim. Account of Cash's during the blitz.

7 Author unknown

8 Author unknown *"Wartime Memories by A Teacher"* Personal account of a teacher from John Gulson School.

9 Author unknown Personal account from Westall, Robert *"Children of the Blitz"* p 126.

10 Author unknown. Personal account

11 Author unknown Personal account.

12 Author unknown (Dick) Personal letter, 18/11/1940.

13 Author unknown (Fred) Personal account based on an article in the *Coventry Evening Telegraph*.

14 Averns, Joan Personal account.

15 Bacon, Dr A H Personal account.

16 Barton, Florence (a) Personal account in *"Images of War" Issue 3, Volume 1.* (b) Tape transcript of her experiences in the Astoria cinema.

17 Bashey, Ministry of Information, hand-written note.

18 BBC Radio transcript of scene in Coventry after November blitz.

19 Bentinck, C D Personal account; tape transcript.

20 Bingley, Joe Personal account.

21 Blackstone, Geoffrey Personal account.

22 Bloomfield, Mary Personal diary; passim.

23 Bramwell, E S Extract from *"The Log Book of the Subversive Enemy Action Squad"* Coventry Record Office Acquisition 629.

24 British Nylon Spinners Letter from the general manager on air raid damage to the Midland regional headquarters.

25 Brooke, H Leslie, GC *"Coventry, 14th November 1940"* in *"The City We Loved"*. He was awarded the George Cross for his services.

26 **Brown, H** Personal account.

27 **Cartwright, W H ,Chief Fire Officer** *"Report on Air Raid Damage Of 14/15 November 1940"*

28 **Castle, E** *"The City Under Fire"* passim.

29 **Chater, Frank** Personal account based on an article in the *Coventry Evening Telegraph.*

30 **City of Coventry** *"Information for the Public Following Air Raids"*

31 **Civil Defence** Report on air raid damage after 14/15 November 1940. NB the figures in this report are often innaccurate and should always be treated with caution.

32 **Clitheroe, Reverend G W** *"Coventry Under Fire".* He was vicar of Holy Trinity Church at the time of the blitz.

33 **Cockerill, Mrs** Personal letter, 15/1/1941.

34 **Compton, S J** Personal account.

35 **Cooke, Reverend Leslie E** *"Public Funeral, &c"* in *"The City We Loved"*

36 **Coventry Motor Spares Ltd** Report of its Voluntary Rescue Squad.

37 *Coventry Standard,* 12 November 1940.

38 **Crichton, Gladys** Personal account based on an article in the *Coventry Evening Telegraph.*

39 **Crump, Alan A** Personal account.

40 **Cunliffe, Marcus** *"The History of the Royal Warwickshire Regiment, 1919–1955"* pp 69–76.

41 *Daily Herald* Saturday, 16th November 1940.

42 **Davis, Martin** *"Every Man His Own Landlord"* The history of the Coventry Building Society; pp 94-5.

43 **Day, John T** *"November Night"* Personal account (1950).

44 **Dudley, Earl of** *"Notes Made by the Earl of Dudley"* He was Regional Commissioner for the West Midlands during the War.

45 **Edwards, Glyn** Personal account based on an article in the *Coventry Evening Telegraph.*

46 **Evans, George** Personal account.

47 **Evans, Ena** Personal account.

48 **Fell, Delia** Personal account; tape transcript.

49 **Fidler, Kathleen; Lutterworth, P** *"The Burning of the Cathedral"* from *"Tales of the Midlands"*

50 **Flitney, C L** *"The Fourteenth of November"* Memories of the blitz.

51 **Garratt, Bert** Personal account based on an article in the *Coventry Evening Telegraph.*

52 **Gas Company** *"Report on Air Raid Damage 14/15 November 1940"*

53 **Gilbert, Harold** *"The Fourteenth of November"* Memories of the blitz.

54 **Goulding, Reg** Personal account.

55 **Griffin, Fred** Personal account based on an article in the *Coventry Evening Telegraph.*

56   Griffiths, M B Personal account.

57   Hall, Ernie Personal account.

58   Hampson, Joyce *"Gone with the Wind"* in *"Equity Life"* pp 28–29.

59   Hancock, B Personal account based on an article in the *Coventry Evening Telegraph*. He was works manager at the Humber, and was awarded the MBE.

60   Harris, D S Personal account.

61   Harrison, G M Personal account.

62   Harrad, M Personal account.

63   Hartley, Alan Personal account.

64   Harvey, Beryl Personal account based on an article in the *Coventry Evening Telegraph*

65   Hill, Joyce Personal account.

66   Hodgkinson, George Personal account; tape transcript.

67   Holmes, Ray Personal account based on an article in the *Coventry Evening Telegraph*. Arthur Butler received a posthumous citation for his bravery.

68   Hopwood, B *"Whatever Happened to the British Motorcycle Industry?"* pp 39 ff.

69   Howe, Ellic *"Bushills of Coventry 1856 — 1956"*

70   Howes, Ralph W (a) Personal account in *"Images of War"* Issue 3, Volume 1; (b) Tape transcript of his experience in the Alvis sales office and as an ARP warden in Hill Street.

71   Hughes, Reg Personal account based on several articles in the *Coventry Evening Telegraph and elsewhere.*

72   Hyde, Marion Letter on behalf of The Queen.

73   Hyde, Councillor Pearl, MBE *"Womens' Voluntary Service"* in *"The City We Loved"*

74   Jackson, B Personal account.

75   Jackson, D H Personal account as an eleven year old at John Gulson School.

76   James, H *"School Life"* Personal account of a seven/eight year old.

77   James M Personal account of an eighteen year old woman.

78   Jessup, K Personal account of her time in the Coventry and Warwickshire Hospital with appendicitis; tape transcript.

79   Jones, Gwyn *"Memories of an ARP Warden During the War"* Personal account.

80   Jones, Mona *"Wartime Memories"* Personal account.

81   Jones, Muriel Personal account in Lancaster and Mason, op cit.

82   Keogh, Joe Personal account.

83   Kimber, Reg Personal account.

84   Lamberti, Nelli Personal account of Spon End and the shelter under the Rudge factory; tape transcript.

85 **Lancaster and Mason** *"Life And Labour in a Twentieth Century City"* Chapter 11, passim.

86 **Lee, Jean** Personal account.

87 **Lees, Jim** Personal letter on events in the Plaza Cinema.

88 **Maddocks, W M** *"The City We Loved"*, passim.

89 **Marchant, Hilda** *Daily Express* report on the scene after the November raid.

90 **Massey, Arthur** *"The Wartime Health Picture in an English City"*; *"Health Department"* in *"The City We Loved"*; *"The Work of the Emergency Medical Services......a Summary"*. and several other reports and letters. Arthur Massey was Medical Officer of Health and head of the wartime Emergency Medical Committee in Coventry at the time of the blitz. He was later awarded the CBE for his services.

91 **Mason-Apps, Goff** Personal account.

92 *Mass Observation* Report.

93 *Midland Daily Telegraph* *"War Diary"* extracts.

94 *Midland Daily Telegraph* (a)Friday, 15 November 1940 (b) 30 August 1941; the citation for Percy Barham and Hubert Jones (c) passim.

95 **Ministry of Information** *"Midland Region Nº 9 ; Minutes of the Full Meeting of the Coventry Committee"* for 1 November 1940 to 4 February 1941.

96 **Muir, A** *"75 Years — A Record of Progress"* on Smith's Stamping Works at Ribble Road and Red Lane; pp73 ff.

97 **National Emergency Committee** *"Notes Made From the Minutes of the National Emergency Committee, 9 May 1939 — November 1946"* passim.

98 **Paul, Bud** *"Sent From Coventry"* pp 95 ff.

99 **Perkins, Nurse Marjorie Eileen** Citation for the George Medal.

100 **Pfleger, J J** *"One Night of Blitz"* Personal account.

101 **Pile, Ernie** Ernie was a journalist for the *Boston Sunday Globe*. This is his report.

102 **Probert, A** *"The National Fire Service"* in*"The City We Loved"* . He was Divisional Fire Officer.

103 **Ramsey, Arthur** *"Bombers' Moon"* Personal account of the dispatch riders of the 12th City Battalion, Home Guard.

104 **Ratcliffe, Captain D W** *"Civil Defence"* in *"The City We Loved"*. He was Chief Warden in Coventry during the blitz.

105 **Reader, Douglas** Personal account from *"Images of War"* Issue 3, Volume 1.

106 **Report** on George Medal recipients.

107 **Rose, R N** Personal account.

108 **Shelton, J B** *"Palace Yard"* in *"The City We Loved"*

109 **Shipley, Joan** Personal account.

110 **Shoesmith, E T W** Personal account.

111 **Shuttleworth, Jessie** Personal account; tape transcript.

112 **Simmons, E** Personal account of the time she worked for the fire service and acted as a part-time firewoman at night in the Central Fire Station; tape transcript.

113 **Smith, J** Personal account; tape transcript.

114 **Stainer, Gordon** Personal account based on an article in the *Coventry Evening Telegraph.*

115 **Tasker, M G** *"Work of the Disposal Squads"* Personal account.

116 **Teers, June T** Personal account.

117 **Thurston, Captain N T** *"Civil Defence"* in*"The City We Loved".* He was ARP Officer and Deputy Controller in Coventry during the blitz.

118 **Tovey, J A** Personal account.

119 **Tugwood, Desmond T** *"The Coventry and Warwickshire Hospital 1838-1948"* pp 60 ff

120 **Turner, Kenneth B** (a) tape transcript; (b) as recorded in *"Images of War" Volume 3, Issue 1.*

121 **Urban, Beryl** Personal account, based on an article in the *Coventry Evening Telegraph.*

122 **Various authors***"Activities of Works ARP Units, 12 October to 15 November 1940"*

123 **Viant, J E** *"The Churchill Connection"* Personal account.

124 **Watch Committee** Minutes of the meeting held on 10 December 1940.

125 **Water Department** *"Report on Air Raid Damage of 14/15 November 1940"*

126 **Watson, I E** Personal account.

127 **Westhead, Elsie P** Personal memories.

128 **Woolley, Jim** Personal account based on an article in the *Coventry Evening Telegraph .*

129 **Zebruski, A M** Personal account based on an article in the *Coventry Evening Telegraph.*

NB Most of the above sources can be found in either the Coventry Central Library's Local Studies section or in the Coventry City archives at Nelson Mandela House, Jordan Well, Coventry.

Index

187

188

189